Immigrants in the United States in Fiction

ALSO BY VICKI ANDERSON

Native Americans in Fiction
(McFarland, 1994)

Cultures Outside the United States in Fiction
(McFarland, 1994)

Fiction Index for Readers 10 to 16
(McFarland, 1992)

Fiction Sequels for Readers 10 to 16
(McFarland, 1990)

Immigrants in the United States in Fiction

A Guide to 705 Books for Librarians and Teachers, K–9

by
VICKI ANDERSON

McFarland & Company, Inc., Publishers
Jefferson, North Carolina, and London

British Library Cataloguing-in-Publication data are available

Library of Congress Cataloguing-in-Publication Data

Anderson, Vicki, 1928–
    Immigrants in the United States in fiction : a guide to 705 books for librarians and teachers, K–9 / by Vicki Anderson.
       p. cm.
    Includes indexes.
    ISBN 0-89950-906-1 (lib. bdg.: 55# alk. paper) ∞
    1. Children—United States—Books and reading. 2. Immigrants—United States—Juvenile fiction—Bibliography. 3. Children's stories, American—Bibliography. I. Title.
Z1037.A54   1994
[PS374.I48]
016.813'54080352069—dc20   94-1231
                                                                          CIP

©1994 Vicki Anderson. All rights reserved

Manufactured in the United States of America

McFarland & Company, Inc., Publishers
  Box 611, Jefferson, North Carolina 28640

Table of Contents

Introduction vii

Annotated Bibliography
(Arranged by Nationality or Ethnicity)

African 1
Albanian 1
Armenian 1
Asian 2
Australian 2
Bahamian 2
Barbadian 3
Belgian 3
Burmese 3
Cambodian 3
Chilean 3
Chinese 3
Cuban 10
Czechoslovakian 10
Danish 11
Dominican 12
Dutch 12
Ecuadoran 13
El Salvadoran 13
English 13
European 15
Finnish 15
French 16
German 17

Greek 21
Guatemalan 22
Hispanic 22
Hungarian 22
Indian 23
Irish 23
Italian 25
Japanese 28
Korean 32
Latvian 34
Lebanese 34
Lithuanian 34
Melanesian 34
Mexican 34
Norwegian 47
Pakistani 49
Peruvian 49
Polish 49
Portuguese 51
Puerto Rican 51
Russian 58
Scottish 63
Senegalese 63
Spanish 64

Swedish 64
Taiwanese 66
Thai 66
Trinidadian 66
Turkish 66

Ugandan 67
Ukrainian 67
Vietnamese 67
West Indian 70
Yugoslavian 70

Appendix: Books Arranged by Grade Level 71

*Nationality Abbreviations
Used in the Indexes* 109

Author Index 111

Title Index 119

Subject Index 129

Introduction

The purpose of this reference book is to enable librarians to identify and utilize fiction books whose main theme is the social life and customs of people who were born outside of the United States and emigrated to the United States. Because of personal interest or a school assignment, readers are frequently looking for information about the physical, social, economic, and other aspects of a foreign culture. This information can sometimes be entertainingly obtained by reading a story of youngsters who are members of that culture. The fiction titles listed herein focus on the daily life and cultural mores of peoples with a lifestyle somewhat different from people who were born in America—the diversity in their daily lives, the hardships they endured and the contributions they made to their adopted country.

This collection has more than 700 fiction titles arranged alphabetically by author within over 60 different nationalities or ethnic groups. The range of reading levels is from preschool through young adult. The copyright dates range from 1965 (and a few earlier) to 1993. The older titles are classics: books that nearly all library collections have regardless of publication date, or books that are still being read by children because of their universal appeal. Some of the books may be out of print, but many of these older titles have been reissued. The material found in this collection covers some historical material as early as 1700, but the emphasis is on contemporary settings.

The selection was broad-based; included are as many titles as could be found that were appropriate to this collection. All of the included titles were found in at least one of the several libraries checked. The titles were not gleaned from *Books in Print* or publishers' catalogs. The books had been read and approved by librarians who had added them to their collection.

In the bibliography there is a brief annotation for each title along with the standard bibliographic information. There is also a grade level specified for each title. The grade designation is a recommendation to help librarians and other users separate picture books and those with different levels of text. Also included are one to three subject headings for each title. These will give the user an idea about what aspect of life the book covers and what kinds of information can be found there.

There are author, title and subject indexes. The title index also specifies the nationality represented by each title. The subject index is intended to help the user find the most specific subject needed. The index is detailed and includes "see also" references. When a subject was represented by a large number of titles, subentries (see the Sports entry in the subject index as an example) or logical subdivisions (see the Friendship entry in the subject index) were used.

Classics, as defined earlier, and "short stories" are not really subjects but are included in the subject index because they are useful.

In each of the indexes, an abbreviated form of the nationality appears with each entry number to make specific searches more convenient. (See *Nationality Abbreviations* in the back of the book.)

There is also an appendix of grade level, arranged by grade, then nationality.

This volume is intended not as a buying guide but as a useful tool in making the most of any collection by allowing accessibility to specific fiction books that fit a reader's needs. This list of fiction books can be used to find stories about other cultures merged into America's heritage. It will also serve as a source of a variety of ethnic material, an expanded subject approach to relevant fiction, and a key to grade level material. It can be used to analyze a collection for balance, to promote ethnic books during ethnic holidays, and to identify and label books of a specific genre.

There are many reasons why accessibility to the fiction about other cultures is important. Colleges are requiring students to create a unit on a multicultural theme for their teaching credentials. Schools in most areas are getting many students from different ethnic backgrounds. The increased interest in the rich variety of Americans' cultural backgrounds creates an urgent need for books with cultural information. *Immigrants in the U.S. in Fiction* will help.

Annotated Bibliography
(Arranged by Nationality or Ethnicity)

AFRICAN

See also SENEGALESE, UGANDAN

1 Sterne, Emma. *Long Black Schooner.* Follett, 1968. Gr. 5-8. A boatload of black captives destined for slavery seized the ship but were tricked into landing it in the United States. (Slavery)

ALBANIAN

2 Drizari, Nelo. *Four Seas to Dreamland.* Pub. Research, 1969. Gr. 5-8. The story of a boy growing up in both Albania and America. (Family; Biography, Fictionalized)

ARMENIAN

3 Cretan, Gladys. *All Except Sammy.* Little, 1966. Gr. 2-4. Everyone in the family is musical except Sammy. He likes baseball but even though he plays well, he feels left out. His discovery of art helps him feel accepted at home and on the baseball team. (Sports/Baseball; Arts & Artists; Music)

4 Cretan, Gladys. *Sunday for Sona.* Lothrop, 1973. Gr. 4-6. Sona goes sailing, which defies her family's code of behavior. Her grandmother goes with her on this first sailing trip. (Women's Rights; Boats & Boating)

5 Kherdian, David. *Asking the River.* Orchard, 1993. Gr. 7-9. A young boy, 13, is an Armenian immigrant. He must cope with his foreign heritage, his parents' wishes and his own wants and needs. (Boys, Teen; Self-Esteem)

6 Kherdian, David. *Road from Home; Story of an Armenian Girl.* Greenwillow, 1979. Gr. 7-9. Veron and her family were deported from Turkey. They faced disease, lack of food, weariness and hopelessness. Veron lost all her family and ended up first in Greece, then America. (Survival; Girls, Teen)

7 Kherdian, David. *Song for Uncle Harry.* Philomel, 1989. Gr. 4-6. Set in the 1930s, this story proves that every kid like Pete needs an Uncle Harry. A good rela-

tionship develops between Pete and Harry. (Friendship; Family)

8 Tashjian, Virginia. *Once There Was and Was Not*. Little, 1966. K-3. Stories that reflect the life of the Armenian people. (Daily Life; Lifestyle)

ASIAN

See also BURMESE, CAMBODIAN, CHINESE, INDIAN, JAPANESE, KOREAN, LEBANESE, PAKISTANI, RUSSIAN, TAIWANESE, THAI, TURKISH, VIETNAMESE

9 Javernick, Ellen. *Where's Brooke*. Children's, 1992. Gr. K-2. Brooke plays hide and seek with her father. She is full of tricks and loves playing with her loving, patient father. (Games; Fathers & Daughters)

10 McDaniel, Becky B. *Katie Can*. Children's, 1987. Gr. K-2. Katie's brother and sister see only what she *cannot* do, but one day she teaches the dog to catch a ball and they see what she *can* do. (Siblings; Girls, Pre-teen)

11 McDaniel, Becky B. *Katie Couldn't*. Children's, 1985. Gr. K-2. Katie is able to be picked up by her father. She is happy that her brother and sister are too big for that. (Siblings; Girls, Pre-teen)

12 McDaniel, Becky B. *Katie Did It*. Children's, 1983. Gr. K-2. Katie, the youngest, is always blamed when things go wrong. "Katie did it" is what she hears. So when mother asks about the flowers... Katie did it. (Siblings; Girls, Pre-teen)

AUSTRALIAN

13 Phipson, Joan. *When the City Stopped*. Atheneum, 1978. Gr. 5-8. A picture of what happens in an Australian town when a general strike hits it and how the children cope. (Working World; Survival)

14 Wier, Ester. *Rumptydoolers*. Vanguard, 1964. Gr. 4-7. A Rumptydooler is a "champion," something top-notch. Digger helps Whit adjust to ranch life in Arizona. Whit came from a snobbish prep school and is unfamiliar with ranch life. (Rural Life; Animals/ Sheep; Boys, Teen)

15 Wrightson, Patricia. *Little Fear*. McElderry, 1983. Gr. 4-6. Mrs. Tucker moves from her nursing home to a rural cottage she has inherited. The local Njimbin lays claim to the henhouse and tries to trick Mrs. Tucker out of the whole place. (Elderly; Crime)

BAHAMIAN

See also WEST INDIAN

16 Prieto, Mariana. *Tomato Boy*. Day, 1967. Gr. 3-5. Davey delivers tomatoes from door to door. His friend is Paco, a Puerto Rican. Davey needs the money for a shirt, Paco needs money for shoes. They need these things for roles in a school show. (Friendship; Loyalty; Moneymaking)

BARBADIAN

See also WEST INDIAN

17 Marshall, Paule. *Brown Girl, Brownstones.* Feminist Press, 1981. Gr. 7- . A family attempting to find a place to live in New York City. (Girls, Teen; Family)

BELGIAN

18 Rose, Anne. *Refugee.* Dial, 1977. Gr. 7-9. Elleke, 12, is Jewish and lives in Belgium in 1939. Her life suddenly changes as Jewish hatred spreads. She emigrates to New York where she has an aunt. (Jews; Girls, Pre-teen)

BURMESE

19 Law-Yone, Wendy. *Coffin Tree.* Independent, 1983. Gr. 5-8. A young girl and her brother, Shan, leave Burma for the United States. They are alone without friends or money. Shan goes mad and his sister has a breakdown. Life in Burma is contrasted to life in America. (Brothers & Sisters; Poverty)

CAMBODIAN

20 Betancourt, Jeanne. *More Than Meets the Eye.* Bantam, 1990. Gr. 7-9. Elizabeth, an American, and Ben Lee, a Korean, like each other but both families object. Then a new immigrant, a Cambodian, heightens the prejudices felt by everyone, including Ben. (School; Prejudice)

21 Crew, Linda. *Children of the River.* Delacorte, 1989. Gr. 7-9. Sundara comes to the United States from Cambodia and wants to be both American and Cambodian. She falls in love with an American boy but must cope with her conflicting feelings. (Romance; Loyalty)

CHILEAN

22 Molarsky, Osmond. *Different Ball Game.* Coward, 1979. Gr. 3-4. An 11-year-old boy moves to California from Chile and finds he needs to make adjustments. (Boys, Pre-teen; Cultural Differences)

CHINESE

23 Anderson, Juanita. *Charley Yee's New Year.* Follett, 1970. Gr. 2-4. To avoid disgrace Charley Yee has to pay his debt of $3.15 before the New Year's celebration ends. (Holidays)

24 Ashley, Bernard. *Cleversticks.* Crown, 1992. Gr. K-2. Ling was having trouble in school because he was "different." One day he picked up a broken cookie by using two paintbrushes, chopstick style. The teacher and the whole class were impressed by this. (Cultural Traits; School)

25 Bales, Carol Ann. *Chinatown Sunday.* Reilly & Lee, 1973. Gr. 3-5. Lilliann tells about her family and how they came to Chicago, her friends in school and her baseball ability. She tells of

holidays, customs and traditions and of life in the Chinese Christian Union Church. (Family; Daily Life; Religion)

26 Behrens, June. *Soo Ling Finds a Way.* Children's, 1965. Gr. K-2. Soo Ling helps her grandfather adjust to modern society. (Grandparents; Generation Gap)

27 Benezra, Barbara. *Fire Dragon.* Criterion, 1970. Gr. 7-9. In San Francisco during the 1906 earthquake Sam is separated from his family. He stays with a Chinese family until he can locate his own. (Earthquake; Family)

28 Bennett, Jack. *Masks, a Love Story.* Watts, 1971. Gr. 8- . When she falls in love with a Chinese boy, a young girl discovers the differences between what her parents have taught her and what they truly believe. (Prejudice; Romance)

29 Buck, Pearl. *Chinese Children Next Door.* Day, 1942. Gr. 3-5. Through the eyes of the sisters Precious, More Precious, and Plenty Precious, American children learn what Chinese life was like before the Communist period. (Sisters; Daily Life)

30 Buck, Pearl. *Chinese Story Teller.* Day, 1971. Gr. K-2. A grandmother tells the children stories just as she had heard the stories told by a storyteller in a village in China. (Grandparents; China; Storytelling)

31 Bunting, Eve. *Happy Funeral.* Harper, 1982. Gr. K-2. A Chinese-American girl, Laura, pays tribute to her grandfather as the family prepares for the funeral in the traditional Chinese way. (Grandparents; Death)

32 Chang, Heidi. *Elaine and the Flying Frog.* Random, 1991. Gr. 2-4. Elaine is the only Chinese-American in her new school in Iowa. She is lonely until she meets Mary Lewis, who loves frogs. (Friendship Among Girls; School; Lonesomeness)

33 Chang, Heidi. *Elaine, Mary Lewis, and the Frogs.* Crown, 1988. Gr. 3-5. When Elaine and Mary Lewis meet, they find they both like frogs. This common interest makes life better for both girls. (Friendship Among Girls)

34 Chao, Evelina. *Gates of Grace.* Warner, 1985. Gr. 9- . Realism, intrigue and romance in the lives of Chinese immigrants. A story of the Wong family in which the father is murdered and Mei-yu and her daughter Sing-hua must survive. (Family; Survival)

35 Cheng, Hou-Tien. *Chinese New Year.* Holt, 1976. Gr. K-3. A chronological description of the events that take place in a Chinese community during the extended celebration of the New Year. An explanation of customs and festivities. (Holidays; Festivals)

36 Chetin, Helen. *Angel Island Prisoner.* New Seed, 1982. Gr. 4-7. A girl tells of the terror she felt when she arrived in America. She was thrown together with hundreds of other immigrants and corralled like cattle at Ellis Island. (Girls, Teen)

37 Chin, Frank. *Donald Duk.* Consortium, 1991. Donald, 12, lives in Chinatown, San Francisco. As he grows up he learns about his Chinese heritage and his role in the family. (Cultural Traits)

38 Coerr, Eleanor. *Chang's Paper Pony.* Harper, 1988. Gr. 2-4. Chang lives in San Francisco in 1850. He wants a pony but doesn't have the money to buy one. Big Pete finds a solution. (West, American; Horses, Trained)

39 Estes, Eleanor. *Lost Umbrella of Kim Chu.* Atheneum, 1978. Gr. 4-6. While Kim Chu, 10, was in the library, her father's umbrella was taken from the umbrella stand. It was valuable because it held important papers. She follows the person she suspected of taking it. (Girls, Pre-teen; Mystery)

40 Evans, Doris. *Mr. Charley's Chopsticks.* Coward, 1972, Gr. 3-4. When a special chopstick is missing from the dinner table, Wu Lin tries to find it before anyone discovers it is gone. (Food; Cultural Traits)

41 Gregory, Diana. *One Boy at a Time.* Bantam, 1987. Gr. 7-9. Wendy is a third generation Chinese-American. She has two boyfriends, both Caucasian, and is deciding which she would like for a steady. She keeps some of her Chinese traditions but for the most part is American. (Romance; Cultural Traits)

42 Haugaard, Kay. *China Boy.* Abelard, 1971. Gr. 6-9. Lee, 17, was sold to America after he lost his family in a flood. He buys back his freedom and finds his sister who was also sold. (Slavery; Flood)

43 Howard, Ellen. *Her Own Song.* Atheneum, 1988. Gr. 4-6. Mellie's adoptive father is in the hospital after an accident. She is befriended by Geem-Wah, a Chinese boy. He knows about Mellie's birth and parentage. (West, American; Adoption; Fathers & Daughters)

44 Keating, Norma. *Mr. Chu.* Macmillan, 1965. Gr. 1-4. Mr. Chu and a young orphan boy look at New York's Chinatown and its celebrations. (Holidays; Orphans)

45 Kingston, Maxine H. *Woman Warrior.* Random, 1976. Gr. 7-9. A Chinese-American woman tells of her life in San Francisco during the 1940s. (Lifestyle)

46 La Rouche, Adelle. *Binkey and the Bamboo Brush.* Beacon, 1982. Gr. 4-7. Benjamin, a Chinese-American teenager, cannot see any reason for studying Chinese. But his grandfather shows him why. (Boys, Teen; Grandparents)

47 Lee, Gus. *China Boy.* Dutton, 1991. Gr. 7-9. Kai Ting was a Mandarin who left China. His mother died, and his stepmother now wants to erase all traces of Chinese culture from his life. (Cultural Traits)

48 Lee, Helen. *My Grandfather and Me*. JACP, 1985. Gr. K-3. A boy and his grandfather go for a neighborhood walk, shop at an open air market, stop at a book store and cafe and go to the park. (Grandparents; Community Life)

49 Lenski, Lois. *San Francisco Boy*. Lippincott, 1955. Gr. 4-6. Through the eyes of the Fong children the reader sees a jeans factory, a Chinese restaurant, a noodle shop, a fish market, a curio shop, a Chinese school, Chinese family life and celebrations. (Daily Life; Community Life)

50 Levine, Ellen. *I Hate English!* Scholastic, 1989. Gr. 2-4. Mei-Mei is from Hong Kong and is learning English. She refuses to speak it and only uses Chinese. She loves China and doesn't want to be American until she learns the benefits of living in the United States. (School; Cultural Differences)

51 Li, Chin-yang. *Land of the Golden Mountain*. Meredith, 1967. Gr. 8- . A family leave their famine-stricken village to work in the California gold mines. Mai Mai, 17, disguises herself as a boy in order to work. (Girls, Mature; Mines & Mining)

52 Lim, Genny. *Wings for Lai Ho*. East/West, 1982. Gr. 3-4. A Chinese girl immigrates to America but is detained for several months on arrival. She tells of the Chinese people detained on Angel Island for years and of their hope to get into the new country. (Girls, Teen; Political Issues)

53 Lo, Steven C. *Incorporation of Eric Chung*. Algonquin, 1989. Gr. 8- . Eric works in the library at Texas Tech University. He becomes involved in a disastrous business venture and learns American business and lifestyles in a humorous manner. (Humorous; Working World)

54 Lord, Bette. *In the Year of the Boar and Jackie Robinson*. Harper, 1984. Gr. 4-6. Shirley Wong comes to America in 1947. She learns English, makes friends and learns to love baseball. She presents the key of P.S. 8 to her hero, Jackie Robinson. (School; Sports/Baseball)

55 Lord, Bette. *Spring Moon*. Harper, 1982. Gr. 9- . Spring Moon's serenely gracious world is sheltered behind the walls of her family's privilege and power. Although she is educated she still lives by traditional bonds. Her daughter rebels. (Family; Generation Gap)

56 McCunn, Ruthanne. *Pie-Biter*. Design Enterprises, 1983. Gr. K-2. Pie-Biter, a weak person, comes from China to America to work on the railroad. He develops a love for pies. He eats so many he becomes strong and earns enough money for passage back to China. (Folklore; Humorous)

57 McCunn, Ruthanne. *Thousand Pieces of Gold*. Independent, 1981. Gr. 8- . Lalu Nathoy, sold to pirates as a young girl in China, then auctioned as a slave, arrives in America. She marries and homesteads in Idaho. Based on a true incident. (Biography, Fictionalized; Slavery)

58 Martin, Patricia. *Rice Bowl Pet*. Crowell, 1962. Gr. 2-5. Ah Jim wants a pet. His mother says he can have one if it can fit into a rice bowl. A description of Chinese family life and Chinatown. (Arts & Artists; Daily Life)

59 Molnar, Joe. *Sherman*. Watts, 1973. Gr. K-2. A 10-year-old Chinese boy, living on Long Island, describes his family life, his school and his hobbies. (Family; School)

60 Namioka, Lensey. *Who's Hu?* Vanguard, 1980. Gr. 5-8. In the 1950s Chinese-American Emma Hu feels out of step in her community, not only because she is caught between two cultures but because she excels in math. (Girls, Teen; Community Life; Cultural Differences)

61 Namioka, Lensey. *Yang the Youngest and His Terrible Ear*. Little, 1992. Gr. 4-6. Recently arrived in Seattle from China, musically untalented Yingtao is faced with giving a violin performance to attract new students for his father, a music teacher. Yingtao would rather be working on friendships and playing baseball. (Sports/Baseball; Boys, Pre-teen)

062 Newman, Shirlee P. *Yellow Silk for May Lee*. Bobbs, 1961. Gr. 4-6. May Lee wants a piece of yellow silk for a grownup dress. She earns and saves her money but when the time comes she has doubts about her decision. (Girls, Preteen; Clothing & Dress)

63 Niemeyer, Marie. *Moon Guitar*. Watts, 1969. Gr. 7-9. In San Francisco, a mystery is solved involving a moon guitar and a Chinese roll painting. Lee Su-Lin is facing a generation conflict within the family. (Mystery; Family; Generation Gap)

64 Pascal, Francine. *Out of Reach*. Bantam, 1988. Gr. 7-9. Jade Wu is a ballerina but her father won't allow her to dance in public. She wins a role in a school production and keeps it secret; she also keeps a secret about her grandparents' laundry business. (Romance; Ballet)

65 Pinkwater, Daniel. *Wingman*. Dodd, 1975. Gr. 1-3. Donald cuts classes in his American school where he feels insecure because he is both poor and Chinese. He goes to the G.W. Bridge where he meets Wingman, a sort of Chinese Superman, who helps him feel important. (Adventure; Fantasy)

66 Politi, Leo. *Mr. Fong's Toy Shop*. Scribner, 1978. Gr. K-2. A toy maker and his young friends prepare a shadow puppet play for the Moon Festival in Chinatown, Los Angeles. (Toys; Holidays; Puppets)

67 Politi, Leo. *Moy Moy*. Scribner, 1960. Gr. 1-3. Moy Moy and her brothers prepare for the Chinese New Year. Celebrations will include the Lion Dance and the Dragon Parade. (Holidays)

68 Reiff, Tana. *For Gold and Blood*. Fearon, 1989. Gr. 4-7. Soo Lee and Ping came to California to look for gold in 1850. Life was not easy but they both endured and Soo went to work for the railroad. (Brothers; Railroads)

69 Reit, Seymour. *Rice Cakes and Paper Dragons.* Dodd, 1973. Gr. 4-5. Marie-Chan lives in New York's Chinatown and sees the Chinese New Year and her other cultural heritages as good. (Holidays; Family)

70 Robertson, Keith. *Year of the Jeep.* Viking, 1968. Gr. 5-8. "Cloud" wanted a Jeep but needed money. Could the gardening service provide the money? (Boys, Teen; Monkeymaking)

71 Ruby, Lois. *This Old Man.* Houghton, 1984. Gr. 7-9. Greta and Wing become friends and Greta meets and likes his grandfather, the Old Man. Greta's mother, a prostitute, has the same plans for Greta but Greta has plans of her own. (Girls, Teen; Friendship)

72 Say, Allen. *El Chino.* Houghton, 1990. Gr. 4-6. You don't have to be Spanish to be a bull fighter. El Chino was a Chinese boy who grew up in the Southwest but went on to be a bull fighter. (Biography, Fictionalized; Sports/Bull Fighting)

73 Stock, Catherine. *Emma's Dragon Hunt.* Lothrop, 1984. Gr. K-2. Emma's grandfather has just come to America from China, and he teaches her the power of the dragons. They cause earthquakes, heat waves, solar eclipses and storms. (Folklore; Grandparents)

74 Tan, Amy. *Joy Luck Club.* Putnam, 1989. Gr. 8- . A story of four Chinese-American women, daughters, mothers and grandmothers. After 40 years of meeting together one of them dies and her daughter takes her place: telling stories, playing mah-jongg. (Mothers & Daughters; Lifestyle; Women)

75 Tan, Amy. *Kitchen God's Wife.* Putnam, 1991. Gr. 8- . Winnie tells of her childhood in China in the 1940s. Only with her personal courage and help from her friends could she endure. (Courage; China)

76 Telemaque, Eleanor. *It's Crazy to Stay Chinese in Minnesota.* Nelson, 1978. Gr. 8- . Eleanor, 17, wants to be an unhyphenated American. She meets Bingo Tang and after a while they want to marry. But their plans fail and she matures in the process. (Romance)

77 Terris, Susan. *Latchkey Kids.* Farrar, 1986. Gr. 5-8. Callie is a latchkey child in a new neighborhood. Her mother works and her father is ill. She must bring her brother home, lock themselves in and call mother each day. She feels like a prisoner. (Girls, Teen; Family)

78 Waters, Kate. *Lion Dancer: Ernie Wan's Chinese New Year.* Scholastic, 1990. Gr. K-3. Ernie performs his first Lion Dance on the streets of Chinatown. There are festival feasts, costumes and rituals of old, as well as the modern dress and technology of 1980 New York. (Holidays; Cultural Differences)

79 Wong, Jade Snow. *Fifth Chinese Daughter*. Univ. of Washngton Press, 1989. Gr. 8- . A story contrasting the traditional Oriental ways and the American ways seen by a girl growing up in San Francisco in the 1920s and '30s. (Biography, Fictionalized; Cultural Differences)

80 Wong, Shawn. *Homebase*. New American, 1979. Gr. 7-9. Four generations of Chinese try to acclimate into American society. (Family; Cultural Differences)

81 Wyndham, Robert. *Tales the People Tell in China*. Messner, 1971. Gr. 4-6. Fifteen Chinese tales that give insight into Chinese customs and values. (Values; Customs)

82 Yee, Paul. *Roses Sing on New Snow*. Macmillan, 1992. Gr. K-3. Maylin cooks a special dish she calls Roses Sing on New Snow for a visitor from China. Even though her father and brothers try to take credit for it, no one but Maylin can make it. (Girls, Teen; Food)

83 Yep, Laurence. *Child of the Owl*. Harper, 1977. Gr. 4-6. In San Francisco's Chinatown in the 1960s, Casey looks for her heritage. She also tries to understand the motives of her father, who is a gambler. (Fathers & Daughters; Grandparents)

84 Yep, Laurence. *Dragonwings*. Harper, 1975. Gr. 7-9. A Chinese father builds a flying machine with the help of his son. It is completed after the Wright brothers finish theirs. A good picture of San Francisco's Chinese immigrants during the early years of this century. (Fathers & Sons; Lifestyle)

85 Yep, Laurence. *Rainbow People*. Harper, 1989. Gr. 6-9. A collection of folktales from Chinese immigrants in the 1930s that focus on their life in the United States. (Folklore; Short Stories)

86 Yep, Laurence. *Sea Glass*. Harper, 1979. Gr. 4-6. Craig makes friends with old "Uncle" Quail who helps him understand his demanding father. Craig and Uncle Quail are both interested in marine life. A small piece of "sea glass" means a great deal to Craig. (Marine Mammals; Fathers & Sons)

87 Yep, Laurence. *Serpent's Children*. Harper, 1984. Gr. 5-8. Cassia is a proud member of the Young clan, Children of the Serpent. She tries to reconcile her father and her brother, Foxfire, who secretly emigrated to America to earn money for his family in China. (Family; China)

88 Yep, Laurence. *Star Fisher*. Morrow, 1991. Gr. 4-6. Joan Lee, 14, and her family find the adjustment hard when they move from Ohio to West Virginia in the 1920s. (Girls, Teen; Prejudice)

89 Young, Alida. *Land of the Iron Dragon*. Doubleday, 1978. Gr. 7-9. Lim Yan-sung, 14, moves to San Francisco and joins a crew of railroad workers. He faces prejudice and treachery. (Prejudice; Railroads)

CUBAN

See also WEST INDIAN

90 Bishop, Curtis. *Little League Amigo*. Lippincott, 1964. Gr. 4-6. Carlos is invited to play Little League baseball and makes friends with the American boys on the team. Misunderstandings occur because of cultural differences but good friendships develop nevertheless. (Friendship Among Boys; Sports/Baseball)

91 Cox, William. *Game, Set and Match*. Dodd, 1977. Gr. 5-8. Charles loves tennis. He meets a tennis coach who gives him lessons. He has trouble at the tennis club because of his Cuban background. (Sports/Tennis; Prejudice)

92 Holland, Isabelle. *Amanda's Choice*. Lippincott, 1960. Gr. 3-5. A story of the friendship between Amanda and Santiago, a Cuban American. (Friendship)

93 Mills, Claudia. *Luisa's American Dream*. Four Winds, 1981. Gr. 7-9. Luisa, 14, meets handsome Travis. She keeps from him her Cuban background and poverty because she feels he will not accept her if he knows. Her friend, Beth, tries to help her with her problem. (Romance; Cultural Differences)

94 Pesera, Hilda. *Cuban Boy's Adventures in America*. Pickering, 1992. Gr. 4-6. Kiki, eight, leaves Cuba for Miami. At first he has problems, then he is placed in a foster home and loves it. He hates to see his parents four years later; he resents poverty and the Cuban ways. (Boys, Pre-teen; Foster Care)

95 Prieto, Mariana. *Johnny Lost*. Day, 1969. Gr. 2-4. Seven-year-old Johnny is always getting lost. He has adventures around the Miami airport and the police station. He is helped by Freedom House. (Boys, Pre-teen; Adventure)

96 Reiff, Tana. *Different Home*. Fearon, 1989. Gr. 4-7. Mario left his family and came to the United States. He has gotten a job and is successful, but he misses his parents in Cuba. He returns to get them. (Family; Careers)

CZECHOSLOVAKIAN

97 Addy, Sharon. *Visit with Great-Grandma*. Whitman, 1989. Gr. K-2. Great-grandmother does not speak much English and Baruska does not speak Czech, but they still enjoy time together baking and looking at pictures. (Grandparents)

98 Barker, Mary. *Milenka's Happy Summer*. Dodd, 1961. Gr. 5-8. Milenka, nine, is a Czech immigrant. She lives on a farm and is lonely until her grandfather comes for a visit. (Lonesomeness; Grandparents)

99 Cather, Willa. *My Ántonia*. Houghton, 1962. Gr. 7- . Ántonia is the daughter of immigrants. She finds a place for herself in her

adopted homeland. She takes on great responsibility running a poor farm, working as a servant and making a better life for herself. (Girls, Teen; Responsibility)

100 Drdek, Richard. *Game.* Doubleday, 1968. Gr. 5-8. Sonny, 12, is given gifts by his uncle but only after a made-up game is played. Later Sonny gives a gift to his uncle and he gets to create the game. A picture of life for Czechs in Cleveland between two world wars. (Boys, Teen; Family)

101 Hickman, Janet. *Valley of the Shadow.* Macmillan, 1974. Gr. 7-9. The view of a 13-year-old boy who witnessed the massacre by Virginians of Moravian missionaries and their Indian converts when they tried to harvest their crops. (Religion; Boys, Teen; Moravians)

102 Kafka, Franz. *Amerika.* New Directions, 1962. Gr. 9- . A young Czech from Prague is having problems adjusting to a new country. (Cultural Difference)

103 Mitchell, Barbara. *Tomahawks and Trombones.* Carolrhoda, 1982. Gr. 2-4. A group of Moravians, living in Pennsylvania in 1755, use music to stave off the Delaware Indians. (Delaware Indians; Moravians)

104 Moore, Ruth. *Christmas Surprise.* Herald, 1989. Gr. 5-8. Kate hates the Indians who killed her parents and kidnapped her brother. She goes to live in a Moravian community and is horrified by their attitude toward Indians. They are busy preparing for Christmas. (Moravians; Holidays)

105 Moore, Ruth. *Distant Thunder.* Herald, 1991. Gr. 5-8. Kate, 15, is a Moravian and thus opposes war. She nurses a soldier during the American Revolutionary War. The reader learns of Moravian life and their choice of pacifism. (Moravians; Religion)

106 Moore, Ruth. *Peace Treaty.* Herald, 1977. Gr. 4-6. A young Moravian boy, captured by Indians, realizes he can use his faith to promote peace. (Religion; Captivities)

107 Skurzynski, Gloria. *Tempering.* Houghton, 1983. Gr. 7- . Andy Stubak, an intelligent ambitious young man, feels strongly about labor practices at the steel mills. He joins a union in Gary and wants to return to Pennsylvania and form a union. Rich in Slovak customs. (Working World; Boys, Mature; Customs)

DANISH

108 Kerr, Helen. *Helga's Magic.* Washburn, 1970. Gr. 3-5. Helga is babysitting for David and Deborah. She talks about Danish life and customs and the special Christmas celebrations. (Holidays; Babysitting; Cultural Traits)

109 Olsen, Violet. *View from the Pighouse Roof.* Atheneum, 1987. Gr. 4-6. Marie, 13, is living through the Depression. The family keeps the farm going after Rosie marries and moves away. Marie misses her but goes on, enjoying some good days but enduring some bad ones too. (Sisters; Depression Era; Rural Life)

DOMINICAN

110 Alvarez, Julia. *How the Garcia Girls Lost Their Accents.* Workman, 1991. Gr. 8- . The girls, after moving to America, fight with Papa over drugs, birth control and love. (Fathers & Daughters; Sisters)

DUTCH

111 De Jong, Dola. *By Marvelous Agreement.* Knopf, 1960. Gr. 7-9. Roza is a Dutch war orphan living in America. She is startled by the change from her orphanage in the Netherlands to apartment life in an American city. (Orphans; Urban Life)

112 Edmonds, Walter. *Matchlock Gun.* Dodd, 1941. Gr. 4-5. Teunis is called to military duty to help stop Indians from raiding Dutch homes. Before he leaves home he gives a large gun to Edward and shows him how to use it. A Newbery book that is still read. (Courage)

113 Gibbs, Alonzo. *Fields Breathe Sweet.* Lothrop, 1963. Gr. 7-9. Gretje, 18, and her father, a Dutch farmer, live on Long Island. They struggle to make a living, and they fight for religious freedom. (Rural Life; Religion; Girls, Mature)

114 Howe, John. *Rip Van Winkle.* Little, 1988. Gr. K-3. The humorous retelling of the story of the man who sleeps for 20 years and finds his town much changed when he awakes. (Cultural Traits; Humorous)

115 Irving, Washington. *Rip Van Winkle and the Legend of Sleepy Hollow.* Macmillan, 1971. Gr. 4-6. Two humorous tales about the Dutch who settled on the Hudson River. (Humorous; Classics)

116 Milhous, Katherine. *Egg Tree.* Scribner, 1950. Gr. K-3. A tradition of the Dutch is to make an egg tree at Easter time. This is a story of how one is made and its significance. (Cultural Traits; Handicraft)

117 Mitchell, Barbara. *Old Fasnacht.* Carolrhoda, 1984. Gr. 3-4. A Dutch boy living in Pennsylvania must be inspired by his "Grossdawdi" to move faster and get things done quicker. (Grandparents)

118 Monjo, F.N. *Rudi and the Distelfink.* Windmill, 1972. Gr. K-2. A Pennsylvania Dutch farm boy describes the major activities of his family each month of the year in the early 1800s. (Lifestyle)

119 Moskin, Marietta. *Lysbet and the Fire Kittens.* Coward, 1974. Gr. 1-3. A story of Dutch colonial life. Lysbet is a little girl who forgets to feed her kittens. (Girls, Pre-teen; Cats)

120 Plummer, Louise. *Romantic Obsessions and Humiliations of Annie Sehlmeier*. Delacorte, 1987. Gr. 8- . Annie comes from the Netherlands to Utah. She attends school and gets along with her sister. But a boy comes between them. (Sisters; School)

121 St. George, Judith. *Shad Are Running*. Putnam, 1977. Gr. 3-5. Corny nearly drowns in the Hudson River and is afraid of water. He needs to help his father with shad fishing. One day two steamboats collide and he must help rescue the survivors. (Fish & Fishing; Survival; Courage)

122 Spicer, Dorothy. *Owl's Nest*. Coward, 1968. Gr. 4-6. Seven stories that provide insight into customs, values and folklore deities of the rural people. (Values; Customs)

ECUADORAN

123 Wainwright, Richard. *Mountains to Climb*. Family Life, 1991. Gr. 2-4. Roberto comes from the Andes with his one-eyed pet llama to live in America. He helps the Explorer Club find shelter on a stormy mountain and rescues their advisor. He leads them to accept a blind boy before they go home. (Adventure; Blindness; Animals/Llamas)

EL SALVADORAN

124 Buss, Fran. *Journey of the Sparrows*. Lodestar, 1991. Gr. 7- . The story of three children who enter the United States illegally from El Salvador. They make their way to Chicago and try to find work. (Siblings)

ENGLISH

125 Avi. *True Confessions of Charlotte Doyle*. Watts, 1991. Gr. 7-9. A story of murder at sea, seen by a girl traveling alone to America in 1802. (Murder; Ships)

126 Beatty, Patricia. *Queen's Own Grove*. Morrow, 1966. Gr. 7-9. Amelia moves from London to rugged California in 1880. She has trouble fitting in and must fight the disease that hits the orange grove. (Girls, Teen; West, American)

127 Breeding, Robert L. *From London to Appalachia*. Thriftecon, 1991. Gr. 9- . Jamie is sold as an indentured slave to a Virginia colonist. He runs away to live with the Indians and establishes a white settlement in the Appalachian Mountains. (Colonial America; Slavery; Cherokee)

128 Bulla, Clyde. *Charlie's House*. Harper, 1983. Gr. 4-5. Charlie is an indentured slave sent from England to America. (Slavery)

129 Bulla, Clyde. *Lion to Guard Us*. Harper, 1981. Gr. 3-6. Three children, without a mother, are headed for America to join their father in Virginia. (Siblings)

130 Chessman, Ruth. *Bound for Freedom*. Abelard, 1965. Gr. 3-6. Two young London boys are sold into bondage and come to New England to settle with a family. (Slavery)

131 Clarke, Mary. *Iron Peacock*. Viking, 1966. Gr. 7-9. Ross McCrae, a Scottish prisoner, and Joanna, who is 16 and fleeing from Cromwell's England, try to build a new life in early America. They are indentured to the Iron Master. (Colonial America; Slavery)

132 Constiner, Merle. *Sumatra Alley*. Nelson, 1971. Gr. 5-8. A 17-year-old boy becomes involved with the British Redcoats and others loyal to the King of England. (Historical Fiction; Boys, Mature)

133 Crompton, Anne. *Ice Trail*. Methuen, 1980. Gr. 4-7. Daniel, 15, is captured by Indians and almost forgets his English background. But he does escape with the help of his Indian friends. (Escapes; Captivities)

134 Finlayson, Ann. *Greenhorn on the Frontier*. Warne, 1974. Gr. 4-6. Harry and Sukey claim their land and build a house. They make friends (Anse and Showanyah) as well as enemies (Simon). Simon is driven out of town and Sukey marries Anse. Harry had been a young British soldier. (Frontier Life; Friendship)

135 Hall, Marjory. *Other Girl*. Westminster, 1974. Gr. 5-8. A family story of colonial America with Quakers and Tories. A romance of a young British girl. (Romance; Quakers; Colonial America)

136 Harris, Christie. *West with the White Chiefs*. Atheneum, 1965. Gr. 5-8. Battenote and his family guide two Englishmen over rough terrain from Fort Pitt to the gold fields of Canada. (Canada; Prejudice)

137 Haugaard, Erik. *Orphans of the Wind*. Houghton, 1966. Gr. 8- . The story of a 12-year-old boy who was a deckhand on an English ship going to America with arms for the Confederacy during the Civil War. (Ships; Civil War, American)

138 Hoguet, Susan. *Solomon Grundy*. Dutton, 1986. Gr. K-3. A story based on the old nursery rhyme. A child of immigrant parents lives in Connecticut and works as a baker. (Daily Life)

139 Ish-Kishor, Sul. *Our Eddie*. Pantheon, 1969. Gr. 5-8. Eddie is the oldest son of the Raphel family. They are Jewish immigrants living in America in the early 1900s. He has a fatal disease and dies. (Jews; Family; Death)

140 Jensen, Pauline. *Thicker Than Water*. Bobbs, 1966. Gr. 4-6. Jan comes to Nebraska during the First World War. Tom and Peggy are not too happy about it. Jan is a skinny boy with British manners and Tom makes fun of him. Jan goes on to prove his worthiness. (Family; Cultural Differences)

141 L'Engle, Madeline. *Other Side of the Sun*. Farrar, 1971. Gr. 9- . A British bride comes to America to meet her husband's family. (Family)

142 Williamson, Joanne. *Glorious Conspiracy.* Knopf, 1961. Gr. 7- . A boy flees the horrors of factory life in the late 1700s. He goes to America and gets involved with the struggle for independence. (Historical Fiction; Industrial Revolution)

143 Wisler, G. Clifton. *This New Land.* Walker, 1987. Gr. 5-8. Richard is a Pilgrim who tells of the miseries his family faced during their first year in "this new land." (Pilgrims; Family)

EUROPEAN

See also ALBANIAN, ARMENIAN, BELGIAN, CZECHOSLOVAKIAN, DANISH, DUTCH, ENGLISH, FINNISH, FRENCH, GERMAN, GREEK, HUNGARIAN, IRISH, ITALIAN, LATVIAN, LITHUANIAN, NORWEGIAN, POLISH, PORTUGUESE, SCOTTISH, SPANISH, SWEDISH, TURKISH, UKRAINIAN, YUGOSLAVIAN

144 Krumgold, Joseph. *Onion John.* Harper, 1959. Gr. 5-8. Onion John is an odd-jobs man, ignored by the community. He becomes friends with Andy and makes a lasting impression on him because of his determination not to change his life. Newbery winner, 1960. (Elderly; Friendship)

145 Reiff, Tana. *Old Ways, New Ways.* Fearon, 1989. Gr. 4-7. Solomon Gold came to America for a better life. But he was unhappy when his daughter wanted to join the theater and his son wanted to marry a non-Jewish girl. (Jews; Cultural Differences)

146 Rosenberg, Liz. *Grandmother and the Runaway Shadow.* Philomel, 1994. Gr. 4-6. Grandmother leaves the Old World for the new America but she is followed by a mischievous shadow. (Grandparents)

FINNISH

147 Adair, Margaret. *Far Voice Calling.* Doubleday, 1964. Gr. 5-8. A lonely boy, Toivo, and his pet seal, Joe Whiskers, befriend each other but the seal must eventually be returned to live among his own kind. (Marine Mammals)

148 Clark, Ann Nolan. *All This Wild Land.* Viking, 1976. Gr. 4-6. Maiju comes from Finland to America. The family face hard times in 1876. They lose their crop and the father leaves and doesn't come back. Maiju and her mother still have the courage to face the future. (Frontier Life; Mothers & Daughters)

149 Cummings, Rebecca. *Kaisa Kilponen: Two Stories.* Coyote Love, 1985. Gr. 9- . Two stories about Finnish immigrants. One relates the time Nattie Kaisa's husband becomes a U.S. citizen, and the other tells about a bothersome boarding neighbor. (Short Stories; Citizenship)

150 Miller, Helen. *Kirsti.* Doubleday, 1964. Gr. 7-9. Kirsti, 16, gets to know her stepmother, learns survival skills and falls in love with a non-Finnish boy. (Romance)

151 Worchester, Gurdon. *Singing Flute.* Obolensky, 1963. Gr. K-2. Hilli comes from Finland to live in Cape Ann. She is fascinated by her uncle's flute, which then disappears. (Music; Mystery)

FRENCH

152 Clark, Ann Nolan. *Paco's Miracle.* Farrar, 1962. Gr. 4-6. Paco and Old Pierre were alone in a French settlement in New Mexico. Some Spanish people came and cared for Paco when the Old One became ill. Paco repays them for their kindness. (Loyalty; Spanish)

153 Crayder, Teresa. *Cathy and Lisette.* Doubleday, 1964. Gr. 3-6. Cathy has a visitor from France, Lisette. They learn from each other about friendship, love and heartbreak. (Friendship Among Girls; Romance)

154 Erdman, Loula. *Room to Grow.* Dodd, 1962. Gr. 7-9. Pierre and Celeste come from France to Texas. They are different from other children and want to become "Americanized" without losing their French heritage. (Brothers & Sisters; Cultural Differences)

155 Field, Rachel. *Calico Bush.* Macmillan, 1931/1987. Gr. 7-9. The story of an orphaned French girl, Maggie, who is "bound out" to a family in Maine in the 1740s. A reissue of an all-time favorite portraying an immigrant's way of life. (Working World; Lifestyle)

156 Hays, Wilma. *Open Gate: New Year's 1815.* Coward, 1970. Gr. 2-4. An American boy and a Creole girl describe New Orleans' French colony in 1812. (Daily Life)

157 Hodge, Jane. *Savannah Purchase.* Doubleday, 1971. Gr. 9- . Two French refugees, exiled from France during Napoleon's reign, live in America.

158 Jackson, Jacqueline. *Taste of Spruce Gum.* Little, 1966. Gr. 5-8. Libby lives in Vermont with French and Italian immigrants who work as loggers. She has to learn to accept them as equals. (Working World)

159 Kerle, Arthur. *Whispering Trees.* North Star, 1971. Gr. 6-9. Stephen Pierce, a French boy, comes to America and settles in Michigan to work in the lumber industry. He makes friends with an Indian boy, Johnny Shawano. (Ojibwa; Working World)

160 Klein, Norma. *Bizou.* Viking, 1983. Gr. 6-9. Bizou, 13, and her mother come to the United States. Her mother immediately abandons her, forcing Bizou to look for friends and family. (Girls, Teen; Adventure)

161 Levoy, Myron. *Alan and Naomi.* Harper, 1977. Gr. 6-9. Naomi moves from Paris to New York during World War II. Alan finds her strange at first, but since they live in the same apartment building, they see each other a lot and soon become friends. The effect of Nazi horrors on survivors. (Friendship; Mental Illness)

162 Murphy, Barbara. *One Another.* Bradbury, 1982. Gr. 7-9. Paul was a French exchange student; Melissa spoke French. They both fell in love for the first time. (Romance)

163 Peck, Robert. *Fawn.* Little, 1975. Gr. 7- . Fawn's father is a French Jesuit. His grandfather was a Mohawk Indian who fought in the wars. Fawn is torn between two conflicting cultures. (Cultural Conflict; Religion; Mohawk)

164 Pundt, Helen. *Spring Comes First to the Willows.* Crowell, 1963. Gr. 7- . Anna's French heritage conflicts with those of her classmates. She realizes that her family values and ideals are good and she is proud. (Girls, Teen; Cultural Conflict; Values)

165 Reiff, Tana. *Chicken by Che.* Fearon, 1988. Gr. 4-7. Che Acsta is a French chef who starts his own restaurant. He has problems with getting and keeping honest help; he also has to cope with a robbery. But he may yet succeed. (Careers)

GERMAN

166 Asher, Carol. *Flood.* Crossing, 1987. Gr. 9- . Eve, the daughter of Jewish-German refugees, finds her values tested when her parents offer refuge to an anti-Semitic family lost in a flood, and when her black friends are hurt by school integration. (Values; Girls, Teen)

167 Baker, Betty. *Dunderhead War.* Harper, 1967. Gr. 4-6. Quince, 17, and Uncle Fritz travel by wagon train during the Mexican War. They endure weather perils, stolen horses, measles and some battles. (War; Frontier Life)

168 Benary-Isbert, Margot. *Long Way Home.* Harcourt, 1959. Gr. 7-9. A German family flee East Germany and come to the United States. They find a home in California. (Family)

169 Colver, Anne. *Bread and Butter Indian.* Holt, 1964. Gr. 4-6. Barbara helps a hungry Indian and a friendship begins. Later Barbara is kidnapped by a strange Indian and her Indian friend comes to her rescue. (Friendship; Kidnapping)

170 De Angeli, Marguerite. *Skippack School.* Doubleday, 1939. Gr. 4-5. Eli would rather do almost anything—fish, carve wood, chase squirrels—than go to school. But when schoolmaster Christopher Dock comes Eli mends his ways and learns to like school. (School; Boys, Pre-teen)

171 Fährmann, Willi. *Long Journey of Lucas B.* Bradbury, 1985. Gr. 7- . Lukas goes with a carpenter crew to America in 1869 to earn money. A storm at sea, a shootout with anti-immigrants, and a race to finish a bridge are some of the events in Luke's new life. (Fathers & Sons; Adventure)

172 Fast, Howard. *Immigrants.* Houghton, 1977. Gr. 7- 9. Dan, born of poor immigrants, rises to become a business tycoon. When the Stock Market Crash of 1929 comes he is badly hurt. (Family; Careers)

173 Fast, Howard. *Immigrant's Daughter.* Houghton, 1985. Gr. 8- . This is book five of a family chronology. Barbara is now 60 years old. She runs for Congress but is defeated. She then goes to El Salvador as a journalist. (Family; Journalism)

174 Fast, Howard. *Second Generation.* Houghton, 1978. Gr. 9- . Dan Lavette and his daughter, Barbara, give aid to striking dockworkers. (Fathers & Daughters; Working World)

175 Fife, Dale. *Walk a Narrow Bridge.* Coward, 1966. Gr. 7-9. A 16-year-old girl and her family move to Ohio and have difficulty giving up their old ways. (Cultural Conflict; Girls, Teen)

176 Fleming, Alice. *King of Prussia and a Peanut Butter Sandwich.* Scribner, 1988. Gr. 4-6. The Mennonites left Prussia because Frederick the Great was forcing them into the military. They emmigrated to Kansas with their wheat seeds. A look at the social and economic history of the Mennonites. (Religion; Mennonites)

177 Fletcher, Susan. *Stuttgart Nancy Mafia.* Atheneum, 1991. Gr. 4-6. Aurora's mother hires Tanja, who is from Stuttgart, Germany, to babysit when she returns to work. Aurora will do anything to get rid of Tanja. (Babysitting; Girls, Preteen)

178 Good, Merle. *Happy as the Grass Was Green.* Herald, 1971. Gr. 9- . A student from a New York university visits Lancaster County, Pennsylvania, to attend the funeral of a friend killed in a demonstration. The reader learns about the customs, values, religion and culture of the Mennonites. (Religion; Values)

179 Gurasich, Marj. *Letters to Oma.* Texas Christian Univ. Press, 1989. Gr. 5-8. Tina, 15, writes letters from Texas to her grandmother in Germany. She tells of her family's struggles to adapt to a new culture while still retaining traditional German ways. (Cultural Differences; Girls, Teen)

180 Hickman, Janet. *Stones.* Macmillan, 1976. Gr. 4-6. Garrett "hates" the Germans during the Second World War. He and his friends persecute an old German man. (Elderly; World War II)

181 Hickman, Janet. *Zoar Blue.* Macmillan, 1978. Gr. 7-9. Barbara is an orphan. She runs away from the Keffer family to find an uncle. John Keffer runs away to join the Union Army. They meet while involved in different pursuits at the Battle of Gettysburg. (Civil War, American; Runaways)

182 Hoff, Carol. *Johnny Texas.* Dell, 1967, Gr. 4-6. Johnny and his family are German immigrants living in Texas. The father and Johnny quickly adapt to their new life, but it is hard for Mama to give up old ways. (Cultural Conflict)

183 Hurwitz, Johanna. *Once I Was a Plum Tree.* Morrow, 1980. Gr. 4-6. Gerry is Jewish and basically nonreligious. A Jewish family from Nazi Germany move in next door, and Gerry begins to think and learn about the Jewish religion. (Jews; Religion)

184 Jordan, Mildred. *Proud to Be Amish.* Crown, 1968. Gr. 4-6. Katie wants to do things that her Amish heritage won't allow. The story shows the social and religious customs of the Amish people. (Religion; Customs)

185 Keehn, Sally. *I Am Regina.* Philomel, 1991. Gr. 4-6. Regina was 10 when she was captured by the Delaware Indians in 1755. But by 1764, after suffering many hardships, she has come to like her captors. She can no longer speak German and has forgotten all her white ways. (Girls, Teen; Captivities; Delaware Indians)

186 Keith, Harold. *Obstinate Land.* Crowell, 1977. Gr. 7-9. The story of a German family, the Rombergs, as they try to eke out a living on the Cherokee Strip. The father freezes to death and the 14-year-old must assume responsibility. (Frontier Life; Family)

187 Kerr, M.E. *Him She Loves?* Harper, 1984. Gr. 7-9. Henry, 16, loves Valerie. She is Jewish and he is German. Her father is a comedian and makes fun of the romance. It becomes a national television routine. (Jews; Romance)

188 Lehmann, Linda. *Better Than a Princess.* Nelson, 1978. Gr. 3-4. Tilli is at last reunited with her mother in America but needs to adjust to this plain-looking, plain-living woman. A gift from her mother of a beautiful doll does this for Tilli. (Girls, Teen; Mothers & Daughters; Dolls)

189 Lehmann, Linda. *Tilli's New World.* Nelson, 1981. Gr. 4-6. Tilli wants to go to school to learn to read but she is needed to help her poor family. She hires herself out as a housemaid and gets to go to school sometimes. The setting is a Missouri farm. (Girls, Teen; Poverty)

190 Leviton, Sonia. *Silver Days.* Atheneum, 1989. Gr. 3-6. The Platt family are all in America. Mama and Papa have jobs and the children learn English. They experience prejudices but have friends and romance. Life is better than they had it in Germany. (Prejudice; Family)

191 Levoy, Myron. *Hanukkah of Great-Uncle Otto.* Jewish Pub. Society, 1984. Gr. K-3. Otto tells of past Hanukkahs and of life in Germany before Hitler. Joshua helps him build a menorah and the family enjoys the celebration. (Family; Holidays)

192 Mannix, Daniel. *Healer.* Dutton, 1971. Gr. 9- . A story of the Pennsylvania Germans' more basic beliefs in hexes, hex signs and the supernatural. (Superstitions)

193 Murray, Michelle. *Crystal Nights.* Seabury, 1973. Gr. 6-9. The Josephs cope with relatives who are refugees from Nazi Germany. Elly, 15, lives in a small town in 1938 and '39 and is trying to hold on to her dreams of becoming an actress. (Jews; Girls, Teen)

194 Reiff, Tana. *O Little Town.* Fearon, 1989. Gr. 4-7. Karl came to America in 1852. He acquires a farm and has a large family but remains a German citizen and keeps German traditions. When his grandson, an American soldier, is killed in the First World War, Karl changes. (Family; Citizenship)

195 Rowland, Florence. *Amish Wedding.* Putnam, 1971. Gr. K-3. The religious customs and ceremonies of a traditional wedding among the Amish. The roles of the bride, groom and all relatives are described. (Religion; Marriage)

196 Selz, Irma. *Katy, Be Good.* Lothrop, 1962. Gr. 4-6. Katy is Amish and used to plain things. She visits New York and sees television, escalators and big stores. Everything is in sharp contrast to the ways of the people in her village. (Religion; Lifestyle)

197 Shefelman, Janice. *Paradise Called Texas.* Eakin, 1983. Gr. 4-6. Mina and her parents leave Germany in 1845 looking for a better life. In Texas they find hardship, tragedy and adventure. (Daily Life)

198 Shefelman, Janice. *Spirit of Iron.* Eakin, 1987. Gr. 4-6. Mina's friend Amaya, an Apache, is captured by the Comanches. Mina disguises herself as a boy and searches for Amaya. (Captivites; Friendship Among Girls)

199 Tobenkin, Elias. *House of Conrad.* Gregg, 1971. Gr. 9- . The story of a three generation family after they emigrated from Germany in 1868. They face problems, adjustments while "Americanizing." (Family; Cultural Differences)

200 Walley, Constance. *Six Generations.* German Village, 1991. Gr. 4-6. Katherine Wolff Beck came from Germany to America in 1850. She was a typical example of the people who lived in the old South End of Columbus, Ohio, now known as German Village. (Community Life; Lifestyle)

201 Weaver, Robert. *Nice Guy, Go Home.* Harper, 1968. Gr. 7-9. A young baseball pitcher, who is Amish, plays for the St. Louis Cardinals. Because he has long hair he is mistaken for a Northern civil rights worker. (Sports/Baseball; Religion; Civil Rights)

202 Weik, Mary. *House on Liberty Street.* Atheneum, 1973. Gr. 7-9. Louis immigrated to America in 1848. The dreams he had did not materialize but he struggled to attain what he thought was of value. A picture of the political, social and economic conditions faced. (Values; Cultural Differences)

203 Weiman, Eiveen. *Which Way Courage?* Atheneum, 1981. Gr. 4-6. Courage is an Amish girl who questions her beliefs. She wants to live in the wider world but doesn't want to hurt her family. (Girls, Mature; Religion)

204 Williamson, Joanne. *And Forever Free.* Knopf, 1966. Gr. 4-6. An immigrant from Germany witnesses the struggle over escaped slaves, the New York City draft riots and the Battle of Gettysburg as he works as a reporter for the New York *Tribune.* (Boys, Mature; Journalism; Adventure)

205 Withey, Barbara. *Serpent Ring.* Dillon, 1988. Gr. 5-8. Jenny lives with a guardian after her father dies. He is not only a refugee from Nazi Germany, he is also a gypsy. (Girls, Pre-teen; Gypsies)

GREEK

206 Aiello, Barbara. *Portrait of Me.* 21st Century, 1989. Gr. 3-4. Christine, 11, has diabetes but can cope with it. It is her Greek heritage she finds difficult. (Illness/Diabetes; Cultural Conflict)

207 Brandenberg, Aliki. *Eggs: Greek Folk Tale.* Pantheon, 1969. Gr. K-3. An innkeeper tries to take advantage of another man's honesty. He thinks he is going to make a lot of money but a lawyer, more clever than he, thwarts his attempt. (Folklore; Values)

208 Foley, June. *Falling in Love Is No Snap.* Delacorte, 1986. Gr. 5-8. Alexandra and Heracles fall in love but both her mother and his father are against them. Should they follow the dictates of their parents, or do what they feel they should? (Romance; Prejudice)

209 George, Harry. *Demo of 70th Street.* Walck, 1971. Gr. 4-6. New York in the early 1900s is an exciting place with a mixture of cultures for young Demosthenes, a Greek immigrant boy. (Boys, Pre-teen; Cultural Traits)

210 Janus, Christopher. *Miss Fourth of July, Goodbye.* Sheffield, 1986. Gr. 9- . Janus tells about his sister, a 16-year-old immigrant who came to America in 1917. The setting is West Virginia. (Brothers & Sisters)

211 Lord, Athena. *Luck of Z.A.P. and Zoe.* Macmillan, 1987. Gr. 4-6. Zach and Zoe hail from Greece. Zach's initials are Z.A.P., which form the basis for the Z.A.P. Club in his rich life. (Boys, Teen; Brothers & Sisters)

212 Lord, Athena. *Today's Special Z.A.P. and Zoe.* Macmillan, 1984. Gr. 4-6. Zach, 11, must take care of his sister Zoe, who is four, and sometimes this and is a problem. The story tells of the problems and pleasures of immigrants. Some Greek mythology and culture are also included. (Brothers & Sisters; Cultural Traits)

213 O'Dell, Scott. *Alexandra.* Fawcett, 1984. Gr. 7- . Alexandra becomes a sponge diver to earn money the family needs because of business failings and a handicapped grandfather. The sponges are a hiding place for smugglers of cocaine. (Smuggling; Elderly)

GUATEMALAN

214 Kingsolver, Barbara. *Bean Trees.* Harper, 1988. Gr. 8– . Taylor is headed west, away from Kentucky where she has no future. In Oklahoma, an abused Indian baby is thrust into her car. She settles in Tucson with the baby she calls Turtle; she meets a Guatemalan couple. (Girls, Mature; Adventure)

HISPANIC

See also CUBAN, ECUADORAN, EL SALVADORAN, GUATEMALAN, MEXICAN, PERUVIAN, PORTUGUESE, PUERTO RICAN, SPANISH, TRINIDADIAN, WEST INDIAN

215 Anderson, Eloise. *Carlos Goes to School.* Warne, 1973. Gr. 3–4. Carlos' first day at school has its ups and downs. (School)

216 Bradford, Richard. *Red Sky at Morning.* Harper, 1968. Gr. 7–9. Steenie and Marcia take in Josh, the new boy in school, as a friend. They teach him how to survive but their ways are very different from what one might expect. (Friendship)

217 Carlstrom, Nancy. *Light: Story of a Small Kindness.* Little, 1990. Gr. 4–6. Seven stories of kindness and its effect on others. (Values; Short Stories)

218 Cisneros, Sandra. *House on Mango Street.* Random, 1990. Gr. 8– . Esperanza is growing up in the Hispanic section of Chicago. She overcomes the poverty and prejudices. (Urban Life; Short Stories)

219 Fern, Eugene. *Pepito's Story.* Ariel, 1960. Gr. K–2. Estrillita has no friends. Pepito is also friendless. They conquer odds to help each other and find that different means special. (Friendship)

220 Holman, Felice. *Secret City, U.S.A.* Scribner, 1990. Gr. 4–6. Two friends from the barrio fix up an abandoned house as a refuge for the homeless. (Poverty)

221 Weiss, Nicki. *On a Hot, Hot Day.* Putnam, 1992. Gr. K–2. A year in the lives of a changing city and the children who reside there. (Urban Life)

HUNGARIAN

222 Anderson, Mary. *That's Not My Style.* Atheneum, 1983. Gr. 7– . John, 16, is the son of Hungarian immigrants who want him to continue the family butcher business. He wants to be a writer. A good story of his growth and understanding. (Writing)

223 Christopher, Matt. *21 Mile Swim.* Little, 1979. Gr. 6–9. Joey Vass is determined to swim across the lake in spite of his "runt" complex. A lot of Hungarian background carries the story. (Sports/Swimming; Cultural Traits)

224 Hinchman, Catherine. *Torchlight*. Little, 1960. Gr. 7–9. Jimmy was an Hungarian freedom fighter. He moves in with the American Windhams. Cindy Windham is very much like Jimmy and they are able to relate to each other. (Girls, Mature; Family)

225 Konigsburg, E.L. *Throwing Shadows*. Atheneum, 1979. Gr. 7– . Miss Szabo is in an old folk's home. She talks about her life in Hungary before coming to America. There are other immigrants in the home, and Philip persuades them to tape their stories for others to hear. (Short Stories; Cultural Traits)

226 Lewiton, Mina. *Elizabeth and the Young Stranger*. Hale, 1961. Gr. 7– . Elizabeth is friendly with an Hungarian refugee girl even though others in her town avoid her; her father also disapproves of this friendship. (Friendship Among Girls)

227 Line, David. *Soldier and Me*. Harper, 1965. Gr. 5–8. Fourteen-year-old Woolcott and Szolda, an Hungarian refugee see a murder take place and fear for their lives. They run away but are pursued. (England; Murder)

228 Tamar, Erika. *It Happened at Cecilia's*. Collier, 1992. Gr. 7–9. Andy is in the ninth grade. He lives above his father's restaurant. All is well until his father "falls in love with a dancer," his cat runs away and the mob threatens their restaurant. (Humorous; Boys, Teen)

INDIAN

229 Mukherjee, Bharati. *Tiger's Daughter*. Houghton, 1972. Gr. 7– . Tata leaves India to go to school in America. She has problems adjusting but ends up marrying an American. She talks about life in India with its poverty and disease. (School; Romance)

IRISH

230 Allan, Mabel. *Bridge of Friendship*. Dodd, 1977. Gr. 4–6. The friendship of a Jewish girl eases the difficult transition period for an Irish family newly arrived in New York. (Friendship; Jews)

231 Bolton, Carole. *Search of Mary Katherine Mulloy*. Nelson, 1974. Gr. 5–8. The adventures of a girl who, after experiencing the horrors of Ireland's potato famine, arrives in New York to search for her boyfriend. She finds that he has just left for the California gold fields. (Girls, Mature; Famine)

232 Branson, Karen. *Potato Eaters*. Putnam, 1979. Gr. 7–9. The O'Conner family left Ireland during the famine of 1846 and came to New York. The mother remained behind and will join her family later. One member of the family has already died. (Depression Era; Family; Famine)

233 Branson, Karen. *Streets of Gold*. Putnam, 1981. Gr. 5–8. Maureen and her family arrive in New York and find life is not easy there, either, and jobs are hard to find if you're Irish. Maureen takes a job as washerwoman. (Working World)

234 Condon, Richard. *Mile High.* Dial, 1970. Gr. 9– . An Irish-American initiates Prohibition and then makes lots of money "rum running," or bootlegging. He builds himself a "mile high" castle in New York. (Humorous; Careers)

235 Conlon-McKenna, Marita. *Wildflower Girl.* Holiday, 1992. Gr. 5–8. Peggy can't find work in her home town in 1850 and sees no future for herself. She goes to America, full of hope and fear. (Girls, Teen; Fears)

236 Cummings, Betty. *Now, Ameriky.* Atheneum, 1979. Gr. 5–8. Briged leaves Ireland during the famine to go to America. She meets poverty and prejudice. But she will win out. She saves money to buy passage for the rest of her family. (Poverty; Prejudice)

237 Curley, Daniel. *Billy Beg and the Bull.* Harper, 1978. Gr. 4–6. Billy Beg is an Irishman who goes around the world doing good deeds for people. (Legends)

238 Fenton, Edward. *Duffy's Rock.* Dutton, 1974. Gr. 5–8. Timothy is an Irish-American searching for his father. The reader learns of Irish family and community life as he follows the search. (Family; Community Life)

239 Fisher, Leonard. *Across the Sea from Galway.* Four Winds, 1975. Gr. 4–6. In 1849 following the potato famine, an Irish boy and his brother and sister are sent by their parents on an ill-fated journey to Boston. (Family; Famine)

240 Giff, Patricia. *Gift of the Pirate Queen.* Delacorte, 1982. Gr. 4–6. Grace needs strength to accept her mother's death and her responsibility to her diabetic sister. A cousin, Fiona, tells of another Grace who was an heroic pirate queen. (Sisters; Responsibility; Biography, Fictionalized)

241 Harris, Christie. *Forbidden Frontier.* Atheneum, 1968. Gr. 7–9. Alison is the daughter of a Scottish trader and a Haida Indian. Megan is the daughter of Irish immigrants. Both girls are rebels, but they both want to see Indian justice. (Scottish; Justice; Girls, Teen)

242 Irwin, Hadley. *Kim/Kimi.* Macmillan, 1987. Gr. 7–9. Kim is Irish/Japanese. She is torn between two cultures. She leaves Iowa and goes to California's Chinese community to help her understand herself. She learns a great deal about Japanese culture. (Adoption; Cultural Traits; Japanese)

243 Lawson, Robert. Great Wheel. Walker, 1993. Gr. 7–9. Conn, 18, comes to America from Ireland. He helps build the first Ferris wheel which appeared at the World's Exposition of 1893. (Boys, Mature)

244 Nixon, Joan. *Land of Promise.* Bantam, 1993. Gr. 8– . Rose, 15, comes from Ireland to join her family. Her father drinks heavily and her brothers are involved in politics in a dangerous way. (Girls, Teen; Fathers & Daughters; Brothers & Sisters)

245 O'Connor, Edwin. *Edge of Sadness*. Little, 1961. Gr. 9- . Father Kennedy tells of the Carmody family, especially Charlie, who is an old miser with family troubles which he confesses to Father Kennedy. A picture of an Irish-American community in Massachusetts. (Religion; Family)

246 O'Connor, Edwin. *Last Hurrah*. Little, 1970. Gr. 9- . The social and political history of Boston's Irish community. Campaigns, elections, city bosses and an Irish wake. (Political Issues; Historical Fiction)

247 Perez, Norah. *Passage*. Lippincott, 1975. Gr. 7-9. Cathleen O'Faolain is with a shipload of immigrants from Ireland where famine is widespread. They are going to America. (Ships; Famine)

248 Reiff, Tana. *Hungry No More*. Fearon, 1989. Gr. 4-7. The McGee family left Ireland after the potato famine of 1850. Mr. McGee finally got on the police force and Mrs. McGee worked as a maid. Life was better for them but it was still a struggle. (Family; Working World)

249 Rowe, Jack. *Brandywine*. Watts, 1984. Gr. 9- . This is a story of hardship, conflict and romance. The Irish-American "powdermen" at an early DuPont chemical plant. (Romance; Cultural Conflict)

250 Sawyer, Ruth. *Roller Skates*. Viking, 1936. Gr. 3-5. A 10-year-old girl roller-skates around New York and meets some of the foreign people who live there, including a produce seller and an Irish policeman. A Newbery winner. (Girls, Pre-teen)

251 Shura, Mary. *Shoe Full of Shamrock*. Atheneum, 1965. Gr. 4-6. Davie's secret dream came true with the aid of an odd little man, a robin's feather and a small green plant. (Family; Fantasy)

252 Stolz, Mary. *Noonday Friends*. Harper, 1965. Gr. 4-6. Twins Franny and Jim live in poverty and each deals with it in different ways. (Friendship; Brothers & Sisters; Poverty)

253 Talbot, Charlene. *Orphan for Nebraska*. Atheneum, 1979. Gr. 4-6. Kevin lives a newsboy's street life until he is sent west by the Children's Aid Society. (Orphans)

254 Yates, Elizabeth. *Hue and Cry*. Bob Jones Univ. Press, 1991. Gr. 5-8. Jared, a member of a mutual protection society whose duty it is to protect the community against thieves, defends his deaf daughter's friendship with an Irish immigrant who has stolen a horse. (Deafness; Justice)

ITALIAN

255 Angelo, Valenti. *Golden Gate*. Viking, 1975. Gr. 5-8. Nino, an Italian immigrant, gives his impressions of America in the early twentieth century. (Cultural Difference)

256 Benasutti, Marion. *No Steady Job for Papa.* Vanguard, 1966. Gr. 7-9. Rosemary's parents were immigrants. Papa found odd jobs where he could. Rosemary works to help support the family. She does go to business college and eventually marries an Irishman. (Girls, Mature; Romance)

257 Bethancourt, T.E. *New York City, Too Far from Tampa Blues.* Holiday, 1975. Gr. 7-9. Tom has adjustments to make as he tries for a corner shoeshine job. His friend, Aurelio, and he form a group and perform for money. They get so good they make a recording. (Music; Urban Life)

258 Bylinksy, Tatyana. *Before the Wild Flowers Bloom.* Crown, 1989. Gr. 4-5. A girl tells of life in a Colorado mining town before the First World War. (West, American; Family)

259 Christman, Elizabeth. *Nice Italian Girl.* Dodd, 1976. Gr. 8- . Anne had an affair in college that she thought was wonderful except now she is pregnant without a husband. She doesn't want an abortion but finds adoption can be a vicious scheme. (Romance; Pregnancy; College)

260 De Capite, Raymond. *Coming of Fabrizze.* McKay, 1960. Gr. 9- . Pictures a community of Italian immigrants living in the Midwest in 1920. (Community Life)

261 De Capite, Raymond. *Lost King.* McKay, 1962. Gr. 9- . A boy grows up in "Little Italy" in Cleveland where everyone works as a laborer. (Working World; Community Life)

262 Di Donato, Pietro. *Christ in Concrete.* Bobbs, 1975. Gr. 9- . Paul's father is killed when a building he is working on collapses. Paul, 11, must also become a bricklayer to support his mother and seven siblings. A story of customs, economic problems and religion. (Boys, Pre-teen; Working World)

263 Di Donato, Pietro. *Three Circles in Light.* Messner, 1960. Gr. 9- . Paolino tells of life in the Italian community in New Jersey during the First World War. Paolino's father dies and Paolino moves from adolescence to adulthood. Some strong sexual passages. (Community Life; Boys, Teen)

264 Dionetti, Michelle. *Coal Mine Peaches.* Orchard, 1991. Gr. K-2. A story of a hard-working Italian family. They have close family ties and are always optimistic. The story is told by a young girl focusing on her grandfather. (Grandparents; Family)

265 Fisher, Leonard. *Letters from Italy.* Four Winds, 1977. Gr. 7-9. Angelo now lives in America but his son, a soldier, is in his old home town of Naples. He reminisces about his boyhood but is thankful to be in America. His son dies in Italy. (World War II; Fathers & Sons)

266 Fletcher, David. *King's Goblet.* Pantheon, 1962. Gr. 7-9. A crippled American boy and a Venetian glass blower are both affected by a pair of beautiful goblets. (Values; Handicapped; Americans in Other Countries)

267 Forgione, Louis. *River Between.* Dutton, 1975. Gr. 9- . Oreste's father is going blind. He is a building contractor in New York. A story of family relationships, adjustments to a new land and the drive for success. (Family; Careers)

268 Granger, Peg. *After the Picnic.* Lothrop, 1967. Gr. 7- . Dudley is about to graduate from high school and doesn't know what the future holds. She likes Rocco, who is of Italian descent and considered a foreigner. (Romance; Prejudice)

269 Gross, Virginia. *It's Only Goodbye.* Puffin, 1992. Gr. 4-6. Umberto, 10, and his father headed for America from Italy. While en route the father was jailed and Umberto had to fend for himself. (Fathers & Sons; Boys, Pre-teen)

270 Jackson, Jacqueline. *Taste of Spruce Gum.* Little, 1966. Gr. 5-8. Libby lives in Vermont with French and Italian immigrants who work as loggers. She has to learn to accept them as equals. (Working World)

271 LeRoy, Gen. *Hotheads.* Harper, 1977. Gr. 7-9. Geneva is the hothead because of her headlong escapades. She copes with old fashioned parents and prejudices against Italian families. (Prejudice; Generation Gap)

272 Mangione, Jerre. *Mount Allegro.* Crown, 1972. Gr. 7- . A story of "Little Italy" in Rochester. Social activities, education and religion are covered. (School; Religion)

273 Marangell, Virginia. *Gianna Mia.* Dodd, 1979. Gr. 7-9. A story of an Italian family of the 1930s and '40s. Eddie hopes to become a lawyer, Paolo a priest, Julio a doctor, and Anna to marry a Catholic. Eddie is killed in the war, Paolo doubts his priesthood, Anna marries a Protestant. (Family)

274 Mays, Lucinda. *Other Shore.* Atheneum, 1979. Gr. 7-9. Gabriella and her mother finally reunite with Pietro, Gabriella's father, in America. She has difficulty trying to be an American until her father realizes that the world is broader than traditional Italy. (Working World; Prejudice)

275 Miles, Betty. *Feast on Sullivan Street.* Knopf, 1963. Gr. K-3. The Italian Festival of Saint Anthony is a big holiday in New York. Michael finds a special way to celebrate. (Holidays)

276 Pagano, Jo. *Golden Wedding.* Random, 1970. Gr. 9- . Luigi left Italy and went to Colorado, married and left for California to attend his parents' fiftieth wedding anniversary. Meanwhile the reader learns about many Italian customs and adjustments. (Cultural Traits; Family)

277 Panetta, George. *Shoeshine Boys*. Grosset, 1971. Gr. 4–6. Tony's father loses his job so Tony goes into the shoeshine business. Tony faces the hazards of doing business in New York City. (Working World)

278 Parini, Jay. *Patch Boys*. Holt, 1986. Gr. 9– . Sammy, 15, lives with his immigrant family in Pennsylvania. One brother is a hoodlum in New York. Another brother is a union organizer. Sammy has the usual growing up problems, including sex. (Values; Brothers; Sex Education)

279 Paul, Louis. *Papa Luigi's Marionettes*. Washburn, 1962. Gr. 4–6. Bessie and Alfred help Italian born Pappa Luigi buy a hot dog stand and retire, not sell, his puppets since puppet shows are no longer popular. (Puppets; Working World)

280 Reiff, Tana. *Door Is Open*. Fearon, 1988. Gr. 4–7. Lina came from Italy to get married and have a family. Her husband's business is successful and she now wants to go to school. She does so and becomes a teacher. (Careers)

281 Reiff, Tana. *Little Italy*. Fearon, 1989. Gr. 4–7. The Trella family landed on Ellis Island in the 1920s. They soon found work and lived in New York City. Their nine children moved to better quarters as they grew up but the parents stayed in Little Italy. (Family; Community Life)

282 Sawyer, Ruth. *Roller Skates*. Viking, 1936. Gr. 3–5. A 10-year-old girl roller-skates around New York and meets some of the foreign people who live there, including a produce seller and an Irish policeman. A Newbery winner. (Girls, Pre-teen)

JAPANESE

283 Bang, Molly. *Paper Crane*. Greenwillow, 1985. Gr. 1–3. A mysterious man pays for his dinner with a paper crane that comes to life and dances. (Fantasy)

284 Battles, Edith. *What Does the Rooster Say, Yoshio?* Whitman, 1978. Gr. K–2. Yoshio, Japanese, and Lynn, American, go to the farm and compare the different sounds animals make. "Ga Ga" goes the duck in Japanese; "Quack Quack" goes the duck in English. In both languages cows say "Moo." (Language Differences)

285 Bonham, Frank. *Burma Rifles*. Crowell, 1960. Gr. 7–9. While fighting in Burma during the Second World War, Jerry learns firsthand the horror of conflict. He is of Japanese descent and uses this to advantage in questioning Japanese officers. (World War II; Burma)

286 Bonham, Frank. *Mystery in Little Tokyo*. Dutton, 1966. Gr. 4–6. Danny and Carol are to take part in the Nisei Festival. But when a stranger comes along and odd things happen, Danny and a police friend try to find out what the trouble is. (Mystery; Festivals)

287 Bonner, Louise. *What's My Name in Hawaii?* Tuttle, 1967. Gr. K-2. A Japanese boy who is about to become a United States citizen in Hawaii learns to love school and chooses a new name from his favorite Hawaiian story. (Boys, Pre-teen; Names; Citizenship)

288 Breckenfeld, Vivian. *Two Worlds of Noriko.* Doubleday, 1966. Gr. 7- . Noriko is adopted. She falls in love with a dental student. Her foster parents give her a four month vacation in Japan. She is concerned about leaving Ken but doesn't want to hurt her foster parents. (Romance; Foster Care)

289 Cavanna, Betty. *Jenny Kimura.* Morrow, 1964. Gr. 4-6. Jenny, Japanese-American, comes from Tokyo to America to visit her grandmother. She meets Alan and both his parents and her grandmother show prejudice. (Prejudice)

290 Charyn, Jerome. *American Scrapbook.* Viking, 1969. Gr. 9- . A story of the relocation of the Tanaka family, Japanese-Americans. All six family members tell their story as they see it. (Family; Internment Camps)

291 Christopher, Matt. *Shortstop from Tokyo.* Little, 1970. Gr. 4-6. Stogie Crane, shortstop for the Mohawks, feels secure in his position on the baseball team until Sam Suzuki of Japan appears on the scene. Stogie is later accused of destroying Sam's glove. (Sports/Baseball; Prejudice)

292 Copeland, Helen. *Meet Miki Takino.* Lothrop, 1963. Gr. 1-3. Miki is chosen to be a Japanese boy in a play even though he left Japan as a young baby. But he doesn't have grandparents and they are to be honored in this play. (Family)

293 Cox, William. *Trouble at Second Base.* Dodd, 1966. Gr. 4-6. There is conflict on a high school baseball team because of the friendship of a Mexican boy and his Japanese friend. (Sports/Baseball; Cultural Conflict)

294 Friedman, Ina. *How My Parents Learned to Eat.* Houghton, 1984. Gr. K-3. Aiko's mother is Japanese and once took lessons in eating with a knife and fork to impress her American boyfriend. Meanwhile he took chopstick lessons to impress her. (Humorous; Cultural Traits)

295 Garrison, Christian. *Dream Eater.* Bradbury, 1978. Gr. K-2. Yukio spares the other villagers from recurring nightmares when he rescues a baku. (Dreams; Community Life)

296 Haugaard, Kay. *Myeko's Gift.* Abelard, 1966. Gr. 4-6. A Japanese girl adjusts to an American school and a life unlike what she knew in Japan. (School; Cultural Differences)

297 Hawkinson, Lucy. *Dance, Dance, Amy-Chan.* Whitman, 1964. Gr. K-2. A story of a Japanese-American folk festival celebration where the children learn the traditions and history of their culture. (Festivals; Cultural Traits; Historical Fiction)

298 Hayes, Florence. *Boy in the 49th Seat*. Random, 1963. Gr. 3-6. A Japanese boy wants to make friends with other boys. He finds a way to get their attention with a humorous twist. (School; Friendship)

299 Houston, Jeanne. *Farewell to Manzanar*. Houghton, 1973. Gr. 8- . A Japanese-American girl tells about life in the internment camps during World War II. The Americans put the Japanese people there for fear of their loyalty. (Internment Camps)

300 Inyart, Gene. *Jenny*. Watts, 1966. Gr. 4-6. An eight-year-old girl learns from her family Japanese customs and arts. She lives like any American girl except she combines these customs with her other American activities. (Cultural Traits; Cultural Differences)

301 Irwin, Hadley. *Kim/Kimi*. Macmillan, 1987. Gr. 7-9. Kim is Irish/Japanese. She is torn between two cultures. She leaves Iowa and goes to California's Chinese community to help her understand herself. She learns a great deal about Japanese culture. (Adoption; Cultural Traits; Irish)

302 Irwin, Wallace. *Letters of a Japanese Schoolboy*. Gregg, 1969. Gr. 9- . Letters written by a Japanese immigrant about his experiences and impressions of America. (Cultural Difference)

303 Kadohata, Cynthia. *Floating World*. Viking, 1989. Gr. 8- . Olivia and her family move around in the 1950s, facing prejudice wherever they go. (Prejudice; Family)

304 Kanazawa, Tooru. *Sushi and Sourdough*. Univ. of Washington Press, 1989. Gr. 7- . A Japanese man goes from California to Alaska during the gold rush. He brings his family from Japan and his son becomes a new American. (Family; Citizenship)

305 Miklowitz, Gloria. *War Between the Classes*. Delacorte, 1985. Gr. 7-9. Amy is Japanese and Adam is a WASP. Both families are against their dating. Then a class project called the Color Game is played where different groups assume different class status. Is Adam changing? (School; Romance)

306 Okada, John. *No-No Boy*. Univ. of Washington Press, 1981. Gr. 8- . A young Nisei boy refused to be drafted into the United States Army because of his strong nationalism. Following his release from prison camp after the war, he was shunned by his community. (Boys, Mature; Loyalty)

307 Okimoto, Jean. *Molly by Any Other Name*. Scholastic, 1990. Gr. 7-9. An Asian, Molly, is adopted by a non-Asian family when she is an infant. She later decides to search for her real parents. (Romance; Adoption)

308 Politi, Leo. *Mieko*. Golden Gate, 1969. Gr. 1-4. A Japanese girl, Mieko, works hard at learning the traditional arts in hopes of being chosen queen of the Ondo Parade during Nisei Week. (Cultural Traits; Girls, Pre-teen; Festivals)

309 Savin, Marica. *Moon Bridge.* Scholastic, 1992. Gr. 4–7. Ruthie, 11, becomes friends with Mitzi, a Japanese-American. Then Mitzi is sent to an internment camp for the next three years. Ruthie's letters are returned unanswered. (Friendship; Girls, Pre-teen)

310 Smith, Doris. *Salted Lemons.* Four Winds, 1980. Gr. 8– . Darby has moved from north to south and has trouble making new friends. One friend, Yoko, is sent to an internment camp (WW II). The other is a German man who is teased by the other children. (Friendship; World War II)

311 Sugimoto, E.I. *Daughter of the Samurai.* Tuttle, 1966. Gr. 7– . The daughter of a samurai came to America and in one generation tried to transcend hundreds of years of tradition and become "Americanized." (Cultural Conflict)

312 Taylor, Mark. *Time for Flowers.* Golden Gate, 1967. Gr. K–2. A brother and sister attempt to sell flowers to raise money to help their grandfather. (Grandparents; Moneymaking)

313 Uchida, Yoshiko. *Best Bad Thing.* Atheneum, 1983. Gr. 4–6. Rinko must spend the summer with Mrs. Hata and her two sons. She has her own ideas about helping a lady she is sure sheh will not like. One disaster follows another. (Girls, Teen; Depression Era)

314 Uchida, Yoshiko. *Birthday Visitor.* Scribner, 1975. Gr. K–3. Emi is tired of eminent visitors and so when one is coming on her birthday she complains. Mrs. Wada tells her she will be pleasantly surprised . . . and she is. (Birthdays; Girls, Pre-teen)

315 Uchida, Yoshiko. *Happiest Ending.* Atheneum, 1985. Gr. 4–6. Rinko's neighbor's daughter is coming from Japan to marry a man she's never met. Rinko wants to stop this but he learns about love and adult problems. (Romance; Cultural Traits)

316 Uchida, Yoshiko. *Jar of Dreams.* Atheneum, 1981. Gr. 4–6. Rinko grew up in Oakland, California, during the Great Depression. Her Aunt Waka from Japan comes to visit, and although the aunt sees the prejudices she inspires the whole family. (Prejudice; Depression Era)

317 Uchida, Yoshiko. *Journey Home.* Atheneum, 1978. Gr. 4–6. Even though they are released from camp at war's end, a Japanese family has difficulty getting resettled. Ken returns from the war wounded and emotionally unstable. Yuki fights poverty and prejudice. (Family; Poverty)

318 Uchida, Yoshiko. *Journey to Topaz.* Scribner, 1971. Gr. 4–6. The story of a Japanese family in California at the outbreak of the Second World War and their experiences in internment camps. Yuki and Ken's father is separated from them. (Internment Camps; Family)

319 Uchida, Yoshiko. *Mik and the Prowler.* Harcourt, 1960. Gr. 4-6. Tamiko makes Mik's life complicated. He takes care of Mrs. Whipple's plants and cats. But now things change and he doesn't know what to do. (Mystery)

320 Uchida, Yoshiko. *Picture Bride.* Simon & Schuster, 1988. Gr. 8- . Hana comes to San Francisco to marry a man she has never seen. This is a story of her life prior to World War II, when she is interned with other Japanese citizens. (Romance; Family; Internment Camp)

321 Uchida, Yoshiko. *Promised Year.* Harcourt, 1959. Gr. 4-6. Keiko, 10, comes to California from Japan. She and Uncle Henry have an uncomfortable relationship because of her pet cat. (Family; Cats; Girls, Pre-teen)

322 Uchida, Yoshiko. *Rooster That Understood Japanese.* Scribner, 1976. Gr. 3-4. Mrs. Kitamura's rooster crows early and a new neighbor complains. Miyo tries to help by placing an ad in the school paper. But Mrs. Kitamura solves her problem in her own special way. (Poultry; Women)

323 Uchida, Yoshiko. *Samurai of Gold Hill.* Scribner, 1972. Gr. 5-8. A young Japanese boy named Koichi and his samurai father head into the California hills in 1869 looking for gold. He notes the differences and similarities between his home and the American frontier. (Fathers & Sons; Cultural Differences)

324 Yashima, Mitsu. *Momo's Kitten.* Viking, 1961. Gr. K-2. Momo finds a little kitten and takes on the responsibility of raising it. It grows up and has five kittens of its own. (Cats; Responsibility)

325 Yashima, Taro. *Youngest One.* Viking, 1962. Gr. 4-5. Momo and Bobby become friends when Bobby finally opens his eyes and sees Momo's smiling eyes. (Friendship)

326 Yoshida, Jim. *Two Worlds of Jim Yoshida.* Morrow, 1972. Gr. 8- . Jim contrasts his life in America with that in Japan; he tells about his two lifestyles and describes the customs that are part of any Japanese-American community. (Biography, Fictionalized; Cultural Differences; Community Life)

KOREAN

327 Beirne, Barbara. *Pianist's Debut.* Carolrhoda, 1990. Gr. 3-4. A young Korean American learns to love the piano as she studies hard and long. (Music)

328 Betancourt, Jeanne. *More Than Meets the Eye.* Bantam, 1990. Gr. 7-9. Elizabeth, an American, and Ben Lee, a Korean, like each other but both families object. Then a new immigrant, a Cambodian girl, heightens the prejudices felt by everyone, including Ben. (School; Prejudice)

329 Choc, Sook Nyul. *Halmoni*. Houghton, 1993. Gr. 4-6. A Korean girl's third grade class helps her newly arrived grandmother feel more comfortable with her new life in America. (Grandparents; Generation Gap)

330 Johnson, Doris. *SuAn*. Follett, 1968. Gr. K-2. An American family is going to adopt SuAn, a Korean. She has been an orphan and wonders about her new mother. (Adoption)

331 Kline, Suzy. *Horrible Harry's Secret*. Viking, 1990. Gr. K-3. Song Lee and Harry are in the second grade where they share friendship, especially after Song Lee introduces her water frog. (School; Friendship)

332 Lee, Marie. *Finding My Voice*. Houghton, 1992. Gr. 5-8. Ellen's parents are trying to make it in America but still cling to their old traditions. Ellen is American and there is conflict with her parents and classmates as she seeks her rightful place in the family and in school. (Girls, Teen; Cultural Conflict)

333 Lee, Marie. *If It Hadn't Been for Yoon Jun*. Houghton, 1993. Gr. 5-8. As she reluctantly becomes friends with Yoon Jun, a new student from Korea, Alice, a seventh grader, becomes more interested in learning about her own Korean background. (Adoption; School)

334 McDonald, Joyce. *Mail-Order Kid*. Putnam, 1988. Gr. 4-6. Flip has a newly adopted six-year-old Korean brother, Todd, and must share his room. He equates this adoption with his own of a fox he ordered through the mail. He realizes they both must adjust. (Adoption; Animals/Fox)

335 Macmillan, Dianne. *My Best Friend, Mee-Yung*. Messner, 1989. Gr. K-3. A Korean-American girl introduces her friend to holidays, customs, foods and family culture. (Family; Holidays)

336 Paek, Min. *Aekyung's Dream*. Children's, 1988. Gr. 2-4. A young Korean girl, Aekyung, is trying to adapt to an American lifestyle while retaining her Korean heritage. (Girls, Teen; Family; Cultural Conflict)

337 Pellegrini, Nina. *Families Are Different*. Holiday, 1991. Gr. K-3. After being adopted a Korean girl finds that all families are different. (Adoption; Cultural Differences)

338 Rosenberg, Maxine. *My Friend Leslie*. Lothrop, 1983. Gr. K-3. Karin, a Korean orphan and Leslie, who is handicapped, develop friendship and understanding. (Physically Handicapped; Friendship)

339 Sinykin, Sheri. *Buddy Trap*. Atheneum, 1992. Gr. 3-6. Cam is Korean and a loner. He is going to Camp Rainbow Lake and is sure he won't like it. His beloved flute is stolen and he becomes a "double agent" in order to get it back. (Self-Esteem; Music)

340 Sobol, Harriet. *We Don't Look Like Our Mom and Dad.* Coward, 1984. Gr. K-2. Eric, 10, and Joshua, 11, are Korean-born boys who are adopted by the Levin family in America. (Family; Adoption)

LATINO *see* HISPANIC

LATVIAN

341 Balch, Glenn. *Runaways.* Doubleday, 1963. Gr. 5-8. Jan is an immigrant from Latvia who starts a new life in Idaho. He gets into trouble and runs away. (Horses, Trained; Runaways)

LEBANESE

342 Shefelman, Janice. *Peddler's Dream.* Houghton, 1992. Gr. 2-4. Solomon goes to America to fulfill his dream. He lives in Texas and is a shop apprentice and then the owner of a department store. He has troubles as well as good fortune. (Family; Careers)

LITHUANIAN

343 Sinclair, Upton. *Jungle.* Doubleday, 1906. Gr. 9- . Jurgis, a Lithuanian immigrant, finds a job at the stockyards of Chicago. He has many hardships which hard work can't overcome. He is in favor of socialism because the labor unions can't cope. (Political Issues; Working World; Classics)

MELANESIAN

344 Goodwin, Harold. *Cargo.* Bradbury, 1984. Gr. 4-6. Wei, 14, comes to New York on a 707 to look for his father. He finds New York very different from Melanesia. (Fathers & Sons; Cultural Differences)

MEXICAN

345 Adams, Ruth. *Fidelia.* Lothrop, 1970. Gr. K-2. Spunky young Fidelia is in the second grade. She is determined to play in the orchestra just as her brother and sister did. She makes her own "cigar-box" violin. (Music; Siblings)

346 Anaya, Rudolfo. *Bless Me, Ultima.* Literacy volunteers, 1976. Gr. 8- . A story of the dignity and traditions of a Chicano community in New Mexico as reflected in the concern for old Ultima, who has the power to do good for her people. She becomes the target of a witchhunt. (Elderly; Community Life; Witchcraft)

347 Anaya, Rudolfo. *Farolitos of Christmas.* New Mexico Magazine, 1987. Gr. K-3. Luz's grandfather is ill and will not be able to light the Christmas bonfires; this will spoil the tradition of the fire lighting the way for the shepherds. She uses candles in bags of sand as a substitute. (Holidays; Cultural Traits)

348 Anaya, Rudolfo. *Heart of Aztlan.* Univ. of New Mexico

Press, 1979. Gr. 8- . All aspects of life merge in an Albuquerque barrio. Clemente is out of work and his family is deteriorating. Crispin helps him understand discrimination and gives him strength to lead his people. (Working World; Leadership)

349 Anderson, Joan. *Spanish Pioneers of the Southwest*. Dutton, 1989. Gr. 4-6. A story of hard work, harsh living conditions and strong Hispanic traditions is told through pictures and narrative during the 18th century in New Mexico. (Family; Lifestyle)

350 Atkinson, Mary. *Maria Teresa*. Lollipop Power, 1979. Gr. K-3. Maria Teresa is having trouble coping with her move to Ohio. Her lamb puppet, Monteja la Oveja, breaks the barrier with the other children in school and she makes friends. (School; Puppets)

351 Babbitt, Lorraine. *Pink Like the Geranium*. Children's, 1974. Gr. K-2. A Mexican-American boy is unwilling to start school until his grandmother changes his mind. (School; Grandparents)

352 Barrio, Edmond. *Plum Plum Pickers*. Canfield, 1971. Gr. 9- . Manuel and Lupe are migrant workers in San Joaquin Valley. A story of their involvement with the camp foreman, their employer, another family of farm workers and a few simple laborers. (Migrant Workers; Friendship)

353 Beatty, Patricia. *Lupita Manana*. Morrow, 1981. Gr. 4-6. Two young Mexicans must leave home and travel to the United States to find work. Their father has died and the moneylenders are at the doorsteps. They must earn money to send home to Mama. (Family; Poverty)

354 Beckett, Hilary. *My Brother, Angel*. Dodd, 1971. Gr. 4-6. Carlos was asked to take charge of Angel while his mother was away. He was 13, Angel was 5. There were problems but Carlos was able to handle them. He is proud to earn his mother's trust. (Brothers & Sisters; Boys, Teen)

355 Beckett, Hilary. *Rafael and the Raiders*. Dodd, 1972. Gr. 5-8. Rafael, 13, comes from Mexico to visit his American cousin in New York. He becomes involved in a robbery at the Metropolitan Museum of Art. (Mystery)

356 Behrens, June. *Fiesta!* Children's, 1978. Gr. K-2. There is a celebration of the anniversary of Cinco de Mayo, the Mexican army's victory over the French army on May 5, 1862. The reader learns about food, plays, dances and crafts associated with the holiday. (Holidays; Handicraft)

357 Bethancourt, T.E. *Me Inside of Me*. Lerner, 1985. Gr. 5-8. Alfredo is orphaned at age 17 when his parents are killed in a plane crash. He is heir to the insurance they had. He feels guilt as well as grief but the money opens many doors previously closed to him. (Values)

358 Bishop, Curtis. *Fast Break*. Lippincott, 1967. Gr. 7-9. Rene is

Mexican and an excellent basketball player. He inspires Sam and they work together. When his visa runs out Sam finds a way for Rene to remain in America. (Friendship Among Boys; Sports/Basketball)

359 Bishop, Curtis. *Little League Double Play.* Lippincott, 1962. Gr. 4–6. Ronnie makes friends with Julian, a Mexican-American. Together they develop a double play combination that's outstanding. (Sports/Baseball; Friendship Among Boys)

360 Blue, Rose. *We Are Chicano.* Watts, 1973. Gr. 4–6. A Mexican student, 12, is enrolled in an all-white school. A story of the lifestyle of migrant farm workers. (Migrant Workers; School)

361 Bograd, Larry. *Fourth Grade Dinosaur Club.* Delacorte, 1989. Gr. 5–8. Juan, Mexican-American, is being teased by other students. His friend, Billy, is afraid to come to his defense. (Friendship Among Boys; Prejudice)

362 Bolognese, Don. *New Day.* Delacorte, 1970. Gr. K–3. A migrant couple have a baby and the whole neighborhood is celebrating. The police come to prevent them from disturbing the peace. Maria's baby is born in a gas station. A Christmas-type story. (Family; Community Life)

363 Bonham, Frank. *Viva Chicano.* Dutton, 1970. Gr. 5–8. A young Mexican-American (Chicano), Kenny, unwillingly breaks parole and must hide because of unjust accusations. (Boys, Teen; Delinquency; Justice)

364 Brenner, Barbara. *Mystery of the Disappearing Dogs.* Knopf, 1982. Gr. 4–6. Elena and Michael have a dog named Perro. One day the dog disappears. While they search for him they run into disco stars, the police, more stolen dogs and criminals. (Mystery; Dogs)

365 Brown, Tricia. *Hello, Amigos!* Holt, 1986. Gr. K–3. Frankie has seven brothers and sisters and today is his birthday. There are traditional meals, songs by a local mariachi group, and the breaking of the piñata. (Family; Birthday)

366 Bruni, Mary Ann. *Rosita's Christmas Wish.* TexArt, 1981. Gr. 2–5. Rosita, nine, waits for the Christmas season to begin so she can see the traditional Pastorelas, or shepherd's play, about finding the Jesus Child. She and her friend, Debbie, take part in the play. (Holidays)

367 Bulla, Clyde. *Benito.* Crowell, 1961. Gr. 4–6. An orphan comes from Mexico to California to live with an uncle. The orphan meets a great artist who changes his life. (Arts & Artists; Orphans)

368 Cardenas, Leo. *Return to Ramos.* Hill & Wang, 1970. Gr. 5–8. Chita leads a boycott in high school. Her father intervenes and the Anglos and Chicanos begin to talk to each other to solve their differences. (Cultural Conflict; Girls, Teen)

369 Chavez, Angelico. *Short Stories of Fray Angelico Chavez.* Univ. of New Mexico Press, 1987. Gr. 9- . Fourteen stories of tragic events, spiritual temptations and moral dilemmas of the Indo-Hispanic people of New Mexico. (Religion; Rural Life)

370 Cisneros, Sandra. *Woman Hollering Creek.* Random, 1991. Gr. 8- . A story of the lives of girls and women living in Texas and Mexico. There are love, sex, revolutions, hardships, family, religion and chores. Included too are young girls, brides, religious women and cynical women. (Family; Women)

371 Clark, Ann Nolan. *Paco's Miracle.* Farrar, 1962. Gr. 4-6. Even though this story takes place near Taos, New Mexico, there are good descriptions of Mexican traditions, customs, clothing and holiday celebrations. (Boys, Pre-teen; Festivals; Clothing & Dress)

372 Colman, Hila. *Chicano Girl.* Morrow, 1973. Gr. 5-8. Donna wants to go to Tucson to learn to be a beautician and earn money. She doesn't believe it when her relatives tell her she won't be accepted in the Anglo community. (Prejudice)

373 Cook, Bruce. *Mexican Standoff.* Watts, 1988. Gr. 9- . A story of drugs and prostitution. The action is in both Los Angeles and Mexico. It is an exciting detective story but does discuss sex, prostitution and drugs. (Drug Abuse; Detective)

374 Cox, William. *Chicano Cruz.* Bantam, 1972. Gr. 7-9. An exciting baseball story conveying the drama of winning and losing, of constant travel and team cohesion. Mando Cruz, Sandy, Jack and Gilbert are the main characters. (Prejudice; Sports/Baseball)

375 Cox, William. *Third and Goal.* Dodd, 1971. Gr. 7-9. A story of football, prejudices, family life and customs. (Sports/Football; Family)

376 Cox, William. *Trouble at Second Base.* Dodd, 1966. Gr. 4-6. There is conflict on a high school baseball team because of the friendship of a Mexican boy and his Japanese counterpart. (Sports/Baseball; Cultural Conflict)

377 Cruz, Manuel. *Chicano Christmas Story.* Bilingual Education, 1981. Gr. K-3. In spite of economic depression Diego and Elenita get their first gifts from Santa Claus. The giving spirit of the family restores the meaning of Christmas. (Holidays; Gifts)

378 Dean, Karen. *Mariana.* Avon, 1981. Gr. 8- . Mariana, 15, is a ballet student. Her father is Mexican Indian and her mother is Russian. She has a fiery temper and must mature before she can experience freedom. (Girls, Teen; Ballet)

379 De Leon, Nephtali. *I Will Catch the Sun.* Trucha, 1973. Gr. 4-6. The story deals with the harsh ridicule Spanish speaking children must endure in school. Raul talks about his family, food, love and fear. He lives in a world of suspicion and hostility. (School; Prejudice)

380 Diaz, Paul. *Up from El Paso.* Children's, 1970. Gr. 7- . Paul tells of his life as a migrant crop worker, his life in the army and the struggle to get an education and escape poverty. He is promoted to police sergeant. (Migrant Workers; Careers)

381 Dunnahoo, Terry. *This Is Espie Sanchez.* Dutton, 1976. Gr. 5-8. After being arrested for running away from home, Espie works for the police as an Explorer Scout. But smuggling and murder are still ahead as Teresa is brought in, very troubled. (Smuggling; Girls, Teen)

382 Dunnahoo, Terry. *Who Cares About Espie Sanchez?* Dutton, 1975. Gr. 5-8. Espie was a loner, running from a bad home. Faced with juvenile hall, or Mrs. Garcia, Espie made the tough decision. (Runaways; Girls, Teen)

383 Dunnahoo, Terry. *Who Needs Espie Sanchez?* Dutton, 1975. Gr. 5-8. Alcoholism is a problem in Espie's life. Her curiosity is aroused by a young girl who befriends her after both are in an accident. (Crime; Girls, Teen; Alcohol Abuse)

384 Dunne, Mary. *Reach Out, Ricardo.* Abelard, 1971. Gr. 4-6. Ricardo, 15, is a poor grape picker but has friends in school and plays baseball. When a strike among workers is talked about Ricardo and his friend Doug fight because Doug is an owner's son. (Migrant Workers; Sports/Baseball)

385 Embry, Margaret. *Peg-Leg Willy.* Holiday, 1966. Gr. K-2. Willy is thankful that Thanksgiving dinner doesn't have to include turkey; especially since Willy is a turkey. (Poultry; Humorous)

386 Ets, Marie. *Bad Boy, Good Boy.* Crowell, 1967. Gr. 2-4. When mother leaves home, problems arise but father lets Roberto attend a children's center where he learns English and makes friends with other children. (Family; Friendship)

387 Fall, Thomas. *Wild Boy.* Dial, 1965. Gr. 4-6. Roberto and his grandfather try to capture a stallion called Diablo Blanco that killed Roberto's father. Grandfather also is killed by the stallion before Roberto finally trains well enough to capture it. (Horses, Wild; Courage)

388 Fernandez, Roberta. *Intaglio.* Arte Publico, 1990. Gr. 8- . Andrea is a ballerina, Amanda is a seamstress, Filomena earns her living in Texas, Lenore is Amanda's sister, and Esmerelda sells tickets at a theater. All of them influence Nenita's life. (Women; Working World)

389 Fink, Augusta. *To Touch the Sky.* Golden Gate, 1971. Gr. 4-6. A 14-year-old Mexican joins the Indians whose land has been taken from them by the Mexicans. This occurs just prior to the Yankees' defeating the Mexicans in the 1840s. (Native American; Land Ownership)

390 Frazier, James. *Los Posadas.* Northland, 1963. Gr. K-2. A story about the Mexican custom of the Posadas. (Holidays)

391 Freeman, Don. *Friday Surprise.* Elk Grove, 1968. Gr. K-2. Mario makes presents at school for all of his family but father gets the best gift of all: Mario's ability to read to him. (School; Fathers & Sons)

392 Fulle, Suzanne. *Lanterns for Fiesta.* Macrae, 1973. Gr. 4-6. Juanita, 12, is a migrant worker in Texas. She wants an education and is determined to get it in spite of all discouraging circumstances. (Girls, Teen; Migrant Workers)

393 Galarza, Ernesto. *Barrio Boy.* Univ. of Notre Dame Press, 1971. Gr. 8- . A story about a home, a family uprooted by a revolution, their escape as refugees and their new life in California. (Family; Escapes)

394 Galbraith, Clare. *Victor.* Little, 1971. Gr. 3-5. Victor goes to a white school, where he hates speaking English. He lives in a Mexican home, where he loves speaking Spanish. He has some problems but on Parents' Night some of them are solved. (School; Language Differences)

395 Garcia, Guy. *Skin Deep.* Farrar, 1988. Gr. 9- . David lived in a Los Angeles barrio. He earned a Harvard law degree and is a successful lawyer in New York City. He is asked by a friend to help an innocent Mexican girl in a blackmail case. (Mystery; Crime; Careers)

396 Garthwaite, Marion. *Mario.* Doubleday, 1960. Gr. 4-6. Mario, 11, is thought to be a "wetback." He picks cotton before he is found to be a victim of circumstances. (Prejudice; Boys, Pre-teen)

397 Gates, Doris. *Blue Willow.* Viking, 1968. Gr. 5-8. The development of friendship between a California family of Mexican descent and an Anglo migrant worker family. (Migrant Workers; Family; Friendship)

398 Gault, William. *Trouble at Second.* Dutton, 1973. Gr. 4-6. Joe was a new player and a Chicano. He was very defensive and not easy to get along with. Mark was the team captain and shortstop; he was determined to pull the team together and win. (Sports/Baseball; Prejudice)

399 Gee, Maurice. *Chicano, Amigo.* Morrow, 1972. Gr. 3-5. Kiki wants to be a cub scout. He latches on to Marc and although they are friends Kiki gets everyone in trouble. An earthquake brings a solution. (Boys, Pre-teen; Earthquake; Friendship Among Boys)

400 Gerson, Corinne. *Oh, Brother!* Atheneum, 1982. Gr. 4-6. Danny is "adopted" by four Chicano teenagers. They inspire him to become a Renaissance man. (Friendship)

401 Gray, Genevieve. *How Far, Felipe?* Harper, 1978. Gr. 1-3. Felipe and his pet donkey travel from Mexico with Colonel Anza's caravan to settle in California in

1775. They face numerous hardships on the way. (Animals/Donkeys)

402 Gray, Patsey. *Flag Is Up.* Nelson, 1970. Gr. 4-6. Pablo lives in a barn at the racetrack. He does odd jobs to support himself and his once famous horse trainer grandfather. They both succeed in life after Silver, a hurt horse, is helped by Pablo. (Horses, Trained; Grandparents)

403 Greene, Constance. *Manuel, Young Mexican American.* Lantern, 1969. Gr. 4-6. A youngster learns how people from various ethnic backgrounds can be American and still observe the customs and holidays of their homeland. (Lifestyle; Loyalty)

404 Griego, Jose & Maestas. *Cuentos: Tales from the Hispanic Southwest.* Museum of New Mexico, 1981. Gr. 7- . These 23 tales provide an authentic view of Hispanic ingenuity and charm. There are stories, legends and myths that portray the wit, wisdom and joy of everyday life in Mexican American villages. (Family; Legends)

405 Hamilton, Dorothy. *Anita's Choice.* Herald, 1971. Gr. 5-8. Anita, 14, is a migrant worker in Indiana. She experiences discrimination, uprootings and heartaches as she moves from place to place. (Migrant Workers; Girls, Teen)

406 Havill, Juanita. *Treasure Nap.* Houghton, 1992. Gr. K-3. Alicia listens to the story her mother tells her about going to grandfather's village. She dreams that she, too, goes there and when she awakes the treasures that the other girl brought back are Alicia's. (Family; Dreams)

407 Hernandez, Irene. *Across the Great River.* Arte Publico, 1989. Gr. 7-9. Katarina and her family are illegal aliens. She tells of cruel labor smugglers and the hardships of poor Mexican families. She also tells of kindness and courage. (Girls, Teen; Poverty)

408 Heuman, William. *City High Five.* Dodd, 1964. Gr. 7- . Mike plays basketball with his friend Pedro who is a student in a bicultural community. (Sports/Basketball; Community Life)

409 Hewett, Joan. *Hector Lives in the United States Now.* Lippincott, 1990. Gr. 2-5. Hector, 10, lives in Los Angeles. A story of his life prior to applying for permanent residency. He and his family face a difficult decision on whether to stay or to return to Mexico. (Boys, Preteen; Decisions)

410 Hewett, Joan. *Laura Loves Horses.* Houghton, 1990. Gr. K-3. Laura lives in California where her father works in a riding stable. She rides Sugar Baby bareback to the creek and then starts riding lessons for her first horse show. (Horses, Trained)

411 Hitte, Kathryn. *Mexicali Soup.* Parents', 1970. Gr. K-2. When the family moved from their village to the city the children kept telling Momma to leave out various ingredients of their favorite Mexicali soup because "city people don't eat them." (Family; Flood)

412 Hood, Flora. *One Luminaria for Antonia.* Putnam, 1966. Gr. 3-6. In spite of poverty and temptation Antonia gets a blessing and a candle for his luminaria. (Holidays; Poverty)

413 Hunter, Evan. *Walk Proud.* Bantam, 1979. Gr. 9- . A violent book about Chicano gangs and class distinctions. A trite book that was made into a movie because of sex and drugs. Some Mexican cultural traits are well explained. (Gangs; Drug Abuse)

414 Jaynes, Ruth. *Melinda's Christmas Stocking.* Bowmar, 1968. Gr. K-2. A small Mexican girl takes her gifts out of a large red Christmas stocking as her parents watch. (Holidays; Family)

415 Jaynes, Ruth. *Tell Me Please, What's That.* Bowmar, 1968. Gr. K-2. Story of two boys, one English-speaking and one Spanish-speaking, as they enjoy a trip to the zoo. (Language Differences; Friendship Among Boys; Animals/Zoo)

416 Jaynes, Ruth. *What Is a Birthday Child?* Bowmar, 1967. Gr. K-2. Depicts the activities involved in a Mexican-American child's birthday. (Birthdays)

417 Krumgold, Joseph. *... And Now Miguel.* Crowell, 1953. Gr. 5-8. Miguel hopes to prove he is responsible enough to help the men with their sheepherding in the mountains. (Boys, Pre-teen; Animals/Sheep; Responsibility)

418 Laklan, Carli. *Migrant Girl.* McGraw, 1970. Gr. 4-6. When one young man in the work crew shows the "Stoopers" that they can stand up for their rights, a 16-year-old girl sees hope for release from the inhumane conditions of migrant workers. The man is Cesar Chavez. (Careers; Biography, Fictionalized)

419 Lampman, Evelyn. *Bandit of Mok Hill.* Doubleday, 1969. Gr. 7-9. Historical novel set in San Francisco in which a young boy finally outlives his hero-worshipping of Joaquin Murietta. (Boys, Teen; Historical Fiction)

420 Lampman, Evelyn. *Go Up the Road.* Atheneum, 1972. Gr. 7-9. Yolanda's family are crop pickers. When her father's brother dies and they go to Oregon to become loggers, her life changes for the better. (Migrant Workers; Working World)

421 Lomas Garza, Carmen. *Family Pictures.* Children's, 1991. Gr. 4-7. A story describing family life in an Mexican-American community in Texas. (Family; Community Life)

422 MacMillan, Dianne. *My Best Friend, Martha Rodriguez.* Messner, 1986. Gr. 4-6. Kathy learns many Mexican traditions from her friend, Martha. She learns new games, nursery rhymes, and the significance of a girl's fifteenth birthday. (Friendship; Birthday)

423 Madison, Winifred. *Maria Luisa*. Lippincott, 1971. Gr. 7-9. Maria Luisa is new in San Francisco; she is staying with relatives until her mother gets well. She experiences her first prejudicial treatment. (Prejudice)

424 Martin, Patricia. *Grandma's Gun*. Golden Gate, 1968. Gr. 4-6. A hidden gun saves the pueblo in Los Angeles. It was concealed by a young Mexican boy to keep it from the invading Americans. (War)

425 Marvin, Isabel. *Josefina and the Hanging Tree*. Texas Christian Univ. Press, 1992. Gr. 5-8. A story rich in Mexican culture. Josefina must save her father from hanging; Maxi's father had been hanged earlier. (Cultural Traits)

426 Marzollo, Jean. *Soccer Sam*. Random, 1987. Gr. K-2. Marco plays soccer better than he can speak English. He teaches all the second graders to play. (Sports/Soccer)

427 Maury, Inez. *My Mother and I Are Growing Strong*. New Seed Press, 1979. Gr. K-3. Emilita's father is in jail. Emilita and her mom are taking his place at the flower garden. Her mother does men's chores but also gains strength and courage. (Mothers & Daughters)

428 Maury, Inez. *My Mother the Mail Carrier*. Feminist Press, 1976. Gr. K-3. Lupita and her working mother share love and respect in a one parent home. (Mothers & Daughters)

429 Means, Florence. *Us Maltbys*. Houghton, 1966. Gr. 7-9. M.J. and Sylly's parents take in five foster children, all girls, some of whom are Mexican or Puerto Rican. The town is upset and against this, but the girls are nice and it works out well. (Foster Care; Prejudice)

430 Mills, Donia. *Long Way Home from Troy*. Viking, 1971. Gr. 7-9. Jeannie is planning to go to college. She falls in love with a "greaser" who drops out of school. (Romance; School)

431 Molnar, Joe. *Graciela*. Watts, 1972. Gr. 4-6. Graciela, 12, is one of ten children; her family are migrant workers trying to better their lives. She tells of her feelings for her older sister, her father's going to school and her brother's illness. (Family; Girls, Pre-teen; Migrant Workers)

432 Mora, Pat. *Birthday Basket for Tia*. Macmillan, 1992. Gr. K-2. Cecelia's aunt is 90 years old and it is her birthday. Cecilia must find the perfect present so she can enjoy all the festivities of this important day. (Birthdays; Family; Gifts)

433 O'Dell, Scott. *Child of Fire*. Houghton, 1974. Gr. 6-9. Manuel is a Chicano gang leader on parole from prison. He wants to prove himself worthy of his Spanish heritage. Ernesto, his friend, also lives in poverty and wants something better. (Gangs; Poverty)

434 O'Dell, Scott. *Kathleen, Please Come Home*. Houghton,

1978, Gr. 7-9. Kathleen's mother accidentally causes the death of her Mexican boyfriend, who was an illegal immigrant. Kathleen runs away to Baja California with her girl friend. (Runaways; Mothers & Daughters)

435 Ogan, Margaret. *Tennis Bum*. Westminster, 1976. Gr. 7- . Chico Gomez, 17, gets a new start when a tennis pro coaches him for tournament play. (Sports/Tennis; Boys, Mature)

436 Ormsby, Virginia. *Twenty-One Children Plus Ten*. Lippincott, 1971. Gr. K-2. All the children in Room 2 thought their class was the nicest until the school bus brought new students from the other side of town. (School; Lonesomeness)

437 Ormsby, Virginia. *What's Wrong with Julio?* Lippincott, 1965. Gr. K-2. Julio, a Mexican-American, refused to talk and share in the class activities. Gradually all the children became aware of Julio's loneliness. (School; Lonesomeness)

438 Paredes, Americo. *George Washington Gomez*. Arte Publico, 1990. Gr. 8- . The Gomez family are adjusting to life in the United States. They live among constant prejudices and hatred as they face conflicting values; they try to be Americans and still keep their heritage. (Family; Prejudice)

439 Paul, Paula. *You Can Hear a Magpie Smile*. Nelson, 1980. Gr. 4-6. Lupe, eight, and her friend, Maria, go to the mountains to look for gold. They get lost without food or warm clothing. They are friends of Manuelita, an herbal doctor, who is being replaced by an Anglo doctor. (Health & Medicine; Girls, Preteen; Loyalty)

440 Paulsen, Gary. *Sentries*. Bradbury, 1986. Gr. 7-9. David is an illegal alien from Mexico who wants to make good in the United States so he can send money home to his family. His story is entwined with Sue, Peter and Laura and they all change. (Short Stories; Boys, Teen)

441 Place, Marian. *Juan's 18 Wheeler Summer*. Dodd, 1982. Gr. 4-7. Juan, 13, is a trucker's helper. He hauls fruits and vegetables in Southern California. He saves the life of his employer after an accident. Juan's father had been killed by a drunk driver. (Courage; Working World)

442 Politi, Leo. *Juanita*. Scribner, 1948. Gr. 1-3. Juanita lives on Olvera Street and is celebrating her fifth birthday. There is the Easter custom of blessing the animals along with other festivities. (Festivals; Birthday; Holidays)

443 Politi, Leo. *Mission Bell*. Scribner, 1953. Gr. 2-4. Father Serra, founder of the California missions, talks about his Indian friends. (Religion; Native Americans)

444 Politi, Leo. *Nicest Gift*. Scribner, 1973. Gr. K-3. A boy living in a Los Angeles barrio is

desolate when Christmas Day arrives and his lost dog still hasn't been found. Tamales are cooked, pinatas introduced, and churros made. Many other barrio life activities occur. (Dogs; Holidays)

445 Politi, Leo. *Pedro, Angel of Olvera Street.* Scribner, 1948. Gr. K-2. Pedro lived in Los Angeles on Olvera Street. This Christmas Pedro was to lead the annual Pasada procession and sing. (Holidays)

446 Politi, Leo. *Song of the Swallows.* Scribner, 1949. Gr. 2-4. Both Juan and old Julian tell about the swallows that come each year to Capistrano. (Birds; Folklore)

447 Politi, Leo. *Three Stalks of Corn.* Scribner, 1976. Gr. K-3. Angelica and her grandmother cook together as grandmother explains the importance of corn and tells Mexican legends. (Food; Legends)

448 Ponce, Mary. *Wedding.* Arte Publico, 1989. Gr. 7-9. A Mexican-American is a pregnant bride-to-be. Her blue collar family does what tradition demands in this case. (Marriage; Pregnancy)

449 Prieto, Mariana. *When the Monkeys Wore Sombreros.* Harvey House, 1969. Gr. K-2. Two brothers go out for the first time to sell sombreros. On their way to market misfortune becomes good luck when an old man teaches them how to clean their soiled sombreros by bleaching them white. (Brothers; Humorous)

450 Reed, Fran. *Dream with Storms.* New Readers, 1990. Gr. 5-8. Juan and Rosa are migrant workers. Rosa dreams of getting an education so she can help her children. Juan objects at first but the education Rosa gets helps them both. (School; Migrant Workers)

451 Reiff, Tana. *Magic Paper.* Fearon, 1989. Gr. 4-7. Lupe comes to California on illegal papers. She gets a job and outstays her visa. She is now an illegal immigrant. She meets Benito and they both work to establish residency before 1982 and get green cards. (Working World; Citizenship)

452 Rivera, Tomas. *And the Earth Did Not Devour Him.* Arte Publico, 1970. Gr. 7-9. As a child turns into a man he goes through wonderment, fear, sadness, frustration and rage. (Boys, Mature)

453 Roe, Eileen. *With My Brother (Con mi Hermano).* Bradbury, 1988. Gr. K-3. A preschooler tells of all the nice things he does with his older brother. A family story. (Brothers; Boys, Pre-teen)

454 Roldan, Fernando. *Kite.* Trucha, 1972. Gr. 4-6. Juanito, a Mexican-American boy, has adventures at school and with his kite. (Adventure; Kites)

455 Roy, Cal. *Serpent and the Sun.* Farrar, 1972. Gr. 4-6. Twelve stories that depict the history, culture, religious life and heritage of Mexican-Americans. (Religion; Cultural Traits; Short Stories)

456 Santiago, Danny. *Famous All Over Town.* Simon & Schuster,

1983. Gr. 8- . Manuel, Gorilla, Hungryman, Pelon and Chato are the Los Jesters. They war with the gang from Sierra Street. Sometimes someone is killed in these fights and someone goes to prison. Can Chato survive this? (Gangs; Urban Life)

457 Schaefer, Jack. *Old Ramon.* Houghton, 1960. Gr. 4-6. An old shepherd is teaching a young boy the business of sheepherding, the secrets of nature and the ways of animals. It is a warm relationship. A Newbery honor book. (Animals/Sheep; Elderly)

458 Schellie, Don. *Maybe Next Summer.* Four Winds, 1980. Gr. 7- . Matt, 17, investigates an illegal alien smuggling operation. He and Shannon have a slight romantic involvement, and the reader gets a view of journalistic life. (Smuggling; Journalism; Boys, Mature)

459 Schoberle, Cecile. *Esmeralda and the Pet Parade.* Simon & Schuster, 1990. Gr. K-3. Juna's goat is named Esmeralda. His friends tell him that she will ruin the pet parade but Juan insists that she will behave. (Animals/Goats; Humorous)

460 Smith, Mary Lou. *Grandmother's Adobe Dollhouse.* New Mexico Magazine, 1984. Gr. 3-5. A tour of a miniature adobe house shows different aspects of the Mexican-American and Native American culture, customs, art and architecture. (Cultural Traits; Housing)

461 Soto, Gary. *Baseball in April.* Harcourt, 1988. Gr. 7-9. These Mexican-American children want to do what all kids want to do: play ball, sing in a band, be in a talent show—and cope with immigrant parents. (Sports/Baseball; Short Stories)

462 Soto, Gary. *Skirt.* Delacorte, 1992. Gr. 4-6. Miata's mother loaned her a very important folkloric skirt to show off at school. She loses it on the bus and the dance is Sunday. She and her friend Ana must find the skirt. (Mothers & Daughters; Clothing & Dress; Dancing)

463 Soto, Gary. *Taking Sides.* Harcourt, 1991. Gr. 4-6. Lincoln moved to a new school where he makes the basketball team. When his new school plays against his old school his loyalties are divided. (Loyalty; Sports/Basketball)

464 Stanek, Muriel. *I Speak English for My Mom.* Whitman, 1988. Gr. 3-5. Lupe's mother doesn't know English so Lupe translates for her. Mrs. Gomez decides she wants to learn English. (Mothers & Daughters; Language Differences)

465 Steinbeck, John. *Tortilla Flat.* Viking, 1986. Gr. 7-9. A classic story with a Mexican-American background. An adventure of three people and their roguish ways. (Adventure; Classics)

466 Strange, Celia. *Foster Mary.* McGraw, 1979. Gr. 5-8. Aunt Foster Mary is a migrant apple picker.

She has many "adopted" children and wants a permanent home. They all settle in Washington and get through the first hard winter. (Foster Care; Migrant Workers)

467 Summers, James. *Don't Come Back a Stranger.* Westminster, 1970. Gr. 6-9. The friendship between a white and a Mexican-American student in college. (College; Friendship)

468 Summers, James. *You Can't Make It by Bus.* Westminster, 1969. Gr. 7- . Paul is a teenager looking for "identity." Lura is a Jewish girl and in love with Paul. The story includes violent gang activities and a trip to Mexico where Paul finds himself. But violence still prevails. (Gangs; Romance)

469 Taha, Karen. *Gift for Tia Rosa.* Dillon, 1986. Gr. K-3. Tia Rosa teaches Carmela, 10, to knit. They share many happy hours together. Then elderly Tia Rosa becomes ill and goes to the hospital. When she returns she gives Carmela a silver rose as a remembrance. (Girls, Pre-teen; Family; Elderly)

470 Taylor, Theodore. *Maldonado Miracle.* Doubleday, 1973. Gr. 4-6. Jose, 12, crosses the border illegally but misses the linkup with his father in California. He works first as a farmhand, then at a mission where he accidentally creates a miracle which only he can explain. (Migrant Workers; Religion)

471 Texter, Sylvia. *We Laughed a Lot, My First Day of School.* Children's, 1979. Gr. K-3. Juan goes to school. He plays with crayons and trucks, sings and dances, plays on the jungle gym, listens to a story and walks home with a friend. (Boys, Pre-teen; School)

472 Trivelpiece, Laurel. *During Water Peaches.* Lippincott, 1979. Gr. 7- . La Verne, 17, comes from a poor family and her father drinks. She wants to go to college to prepare for a better life. She has a romance with a Mexican university student. (Romance; Girls, Teen)

473 Van Der Veer, Judy. *Hold the Rein Free.* Golden Gate, 1966. Gr. 7-9. Kiki, a Mexican-American boy, and his friend, Army, hide a horse so its unborn foal will not be destroyed by its owner. (Horses, Trained)

474 Vasquez, Richard. *Chicano.* Doubleday, 1971. Gr. 9- . The Sandoval family has problems of adjustment and discrimination but also the joy of family and romance in the Latin barrio in Los Angeles. (Family; Prejudice; Romance)

475 Villarreal, Jose. *Pocho.* Doubleday, 1976. Gr. 7-9. Richard was raised during the Depression. He is the oldest son of a migrant worker working in Santa Clara, California. (Depression Era; Migrant Workers)

476 Warren, Mary. *Shadow of the Valley.* Westminster, 1967. Gr. 5-8. A black VISTA volunteer, staying with her family, introduces an Oregon high school senior to a world and to opinions which she had not thought concerned her. (Prejudice; Girls, Teen; Afro-Americans)

477 Whitney, Phyllis. *Long Time Coming.* New American, 1976. Gr. 6-9. Christie's father owns a canning factory that employs migrant workers. She finds herself in the middle of a discrimination situation. (Migrant Workers; Prejudice)

478 Williams, Vera. *Chair for My Mother.* Greenwillow, 1982. Gr. K-2. A child, her waitress mother and her grandmother save what money they can to buy a comfortable chair after their furniture is lost in a fire. (Family; Poverty)

479 Williams, Vera. *Music, Music for Everyone.* Greenwillow, 1984. Gr. K-2. Rosa plays her accordion with her friends in the Oak Street Band and earns money to help her mother with expenses while her grandmother is sick. (Family; Music)

480 Williams, Vera. *Something Special for Me.* Greenwillow, 1983. Gr. K-2. Rosa has difficulty choosing a special birthday present to buy with the money her mother and grandmother have saved, until she hears a man playing an accordion. (Family; Birthday)

481 Williams, Vera. *Stringbean's Trip to the Shining Sea.* Greenwillow, 1988. Gr. 1-4. Stringbean and his brother Fred drive to the Pacific and send cards home to their family. The cards show nature, tourist and historic spots. There is much to this book as one goes along. (Brothers; Adventure)

482 Wolf, Bernard. *In This Proud Land.* Lippincott, 1978. Gr. 4-5. A Mexican-American migrant worker family, the Hernandezes, live in Texas but work in Minnesota on a sugar beet farm. Pride, family devotion, fatigue and poverty are part of everyday life. (Migrant Workers; Poverty)

483 Young, Bob. *Across the Tracks.* Messner, 1958. Gr. 7-9. Betty is a happy girl with good grades in school who wins a scholarship to college. A story of a middle-class Mexican-American family and an average teenage girl. (Girls, Teen)

484 Young, Bob. *Good-bye, Amigos.* Messner, 1963. Gr. 5-8. Cathy, a rancher's daughter, tries to better working conditions of migrant workers with unforeseen results. (Migrant Workers)

NORWEGIAN

485 Anderson, Mary. *Who Says Nobody's Perfect?* Delacorte, 1987. Gr. 7- . Ingvild is an exchange student from Norway. She excels in everything. Jenny and her friend, Lisa, plan self improvement so as to compete. It all ends well. (Girls, Teen; Jealousy)

486 Archer, Marion. *There Is a Happy Land.* Whitman, 1963. Gr. 4-6. Signe's parents move to America. She doesn't go with them but joins them later. She finds them very changed and not for the better. (Family)

487 Bojer, Johan. *Emigrants.* Greenwood, 1974. Gr. 9- . A family leaves Norway and comes to North Dakota. The parents save money and later return to Norway, but the children have become "Americanized" and want to stay in America. (Family; Generation Gap)

488 Cather, Willa. *O Pioneers!* Houghton, 1941. Gr. 7- . The Bergsen family live in Nebraska. They have difficulties adjusting to a new country, new ways to make a living, a new language, and new customs. (Family; Cultural Differences)

489 Dahl, Borghild. *Good News.* Dutton, 1966. Gr. 6-9. Two girls decide to publish a weekly newspaper in their town as a college assignment. They describe a Midwestern town with a large Norwegian population. (Daily Life; Community Life)

490 Dahl, Borghild. *Homecoming.* Dutton, 1960. Gr. 7-9. Lyng rebels against her parents' customs and wants to be American like her friends. When she graduates from college she wants to teach. There is generational conflict as well as cultural. (Cultural Conflict; Generation Gap)

491 Dahl, Borghild. *Under This Roof.* Dutton, 1961. Gr. 5-8. Kristine's parents die and she tries to keep the family together in spite of a cold winter and its hardships. (Family)

492 Forbes, Kathryn. *Mama's Bank Account.* Harcourt, 1968. Gr. 8- . Mama guided her immigrant family through the hardships of settling in a new country. (Family)

493 Paulsen, Gary. *Winter Room.* Orchard, 1989. Gr. 5-8. A boy's life on a Minnesota farm with his Norwegian uncle. (Rural Life)

494 Reiff, Tana. *Push to the West.* Fearon, 1989. Gr. 4-7. Lars and Karin come to Minnesota and stay with relatives. They start farming but locusts and severe winters hamper them. When other Norwegian families come to the area they are more content. (Rural Life)

495 Rolvaag, Ole. *Boat of Longing.* Greenwood, 1974. Gr. 7- . Nils leaves Norway and writes home to his parents. When he stops writing, his father goes to find him but is stopped at Ellis Island. He goes home and invents a story for his wife that all is well. (Family)

496 Rolvaag, Ole. *Their Father's God.* Greenwood, 1974. Gr. 9- . Peder is Norwegian and marries Susie, an Irish Catholic. There is too deep a difference in religious tolerance for the marriage to succeed. (Marriage; Religion)

497 Rolvaag, Ole. *Third Life of Per Smevik.* Dillon, 1971. Gr. 9- . Peter is unaccustomed to American ways. A description of South Dakota as seen through the eyes of a foreigner in the 1900s as he writes letters home to Norway. (Rural Life; Cultural Differences)

Pakistani

498 Andrews, Jean. *Secret in the Dorm Attic.* Gallaudet Univ. Press, 1990. Gr. 4-6. Saleen joins Matt at the school for the deaf. There, along with hearing friend Donald, Matt investigates a mystery with Saleen as a suspect. (Deafness; Mystery)

499 Parker, Richard. *Boy Who Wasn't Lonely.* Bobbs, 1965. Gr. 4-6. Cricket meets a Pakistani girl and learns about true friendship and happiness. (Friendship)

Peruvian

500 Molloy, Anne. *Girl from Two Miles High.* Hastings House, 1967. Gr. 4-6. After her father's death in Peru a young girl, Phoebe, must adjust to living with her grandparents on the coast of Maine. (Girls, Pre-teen; Grandparents)

Polish

501 Algren, Nelson. *Neon Wilderness.* Peter Smith, 1969. Gr. 9- . Short stories describe the hardships of life on Chicago's West Side as new immigrants were being acculturated. (Family; Short Stories)

502 Asch, Sholem. *Mother.* AMS, 1970. Gr. 7- . Mother is the center of the family that emigrated from Poland to America. After she dies, everything goes wrong until the older daughter comes to help raise the younger children. (Mothers & Daughters; Jews)

503 Burt, Katherine. *Strong Citadel.* New American, 1975. Gr. 9- . Katia Polenov is found to be wise and understanding when the daughter of Judge Evarts is disillusioned. (Girls, Teen)

504 Chase, Mary. *Journey to Boston.* Norton, 1965. Gr. 5-8. The story of Polish immigrants living in Massachusetts. They work hard on their farms and sell their produce in Boston. (Family; Boys, Teen)

505 Estes, Eleanor. *Hundred Dresses.* Harcourt, 1944. Gr. 4-6. A poor Polish girl tells her classmates she has a hundred dresses at home. They ridicule her because she always wears the same faded dress. It is her drawings she's talking about, and she wins an award. (Arts & Artists; Poverty)

506 Evernden, Margery. *Dream Keeper.* Lothrop, 1985. Gr. 5-8. Becka learns of her grandmother's immigration to America from a Jewish shtetl in Poland when she finds a tape telling about the Russian army conscription. (Grandparents)

507 Fineman, Irving. *Hear, Ye Sons.* Longman's, 1975. Gr. 9- . A successful Polish immigrant tells of life in the Jewish ghettos in both Poland and the United States. The story gives insights into the Jewish heritage and tradition, family customs and values. (Values; Daily Life)

508 Holman, Felice. *Murderer.* Scribner, 1978. Gr. 4-6. Hershy lives in Pennsylvania during the

Great Depression. He is Jewish and lives in a Polish town. He must contend with all the prejudices. (Jews; Depression Era; Prejudice)

509 Hotze, Sollace. *Summer Endings.* Clarion, 1991. Gr. 5-8. Christine, 12, and her sister and mother left Poland six years ago. The two sisters now await their politically active father, whom they left behind. (Fathers; Family)

510 Janney, Russell. *Miracle of the Bells.* Prentice, 1973. Gr. 7- . A Polish girl is in Hollywood and about to become a big star when she meets an untimely death. The man that loved her is the one who experiences the "miracle of the bells." (Romance; Girls, Mature)

511 Kushner, Donn. *Uncle Jacob's Ghost Story.* Holt, 1986. Gr. 4-6. Great Uncle Jacob was the black sheep of Paul's family. He believed that the ghosts of two close friends followed him from Poland to America. (Family; Ghosts)

512 Leighton, Maxinne. *Ellis Island Christmas.* Viking, 1992. Gr. K-3. Krysia left Poland to join her father in America. She arrives at Ellis Island on Christmas Eve. (Holidays)

513 Lenski, Lois. *We Live in the North.* Lippincott, 1965. Gr. K-3. Joseph's dad works at an auto plant in Detroit. The houses in his neighborhood are all painted white and have nice green gardens. Several short stories about Polish customs and the feeling of being in America. (Short Stories; Cultural Traits)

514 Mark, Michael. *Toba at the Hands of a Thief.* Bradbury, 1985. Gr. 7- . Toba is a Jewish girl who leaves Poland to join her sister in America. (Jews; Sisters)

515 Pellowski, Anne. *Betsy's Up-and-Down Year.* Philomel, 1983. Gr. 4-6. This is Betsy's story about life on the farm. She experiences jealousy among her brothers and sisters and sadness as older members of the family die. (Girls, Teen; Family)

516 Pellowski, Anne. *First Farm in the Valley: Anna's Story.* Philomel, 1982. Gr. 5-8. Anna is the first in her family to be born in America and the first to own a farm in Wisconsin. But she dreams of returning to Poland. (Girls, Teen; Rural Life)

517 Pellowski, Anne. *Stairstep Farm: Anna Rose's Story.* Philomel, 1981. Gr. 5-8. Anna Rose is part of the third generation to grow up on the farm. She enjoys the work with her sisters and brothers but she wants to go to school. (Girls, Teen; Rural Life)

518 Pellowski, Anne. *Willow Wind Farm: Betsy's Story.* Philomel, 1981. Gr. 4-6. Betsy is the granddaughter of Annie. She is one of ten children and is surrounded by family and extended family. (Girls, Teen; Rural Life)

519 Pellowski, Anne. *Winding Valley Farm: Annie's Story.* Philomel, 1982. Gr. 5-8. Annie loved the farm and didn't want to move to the city. When the accident occurred she knew that she would not be leaving the farm. (Girls, Teen; Rural Life)

520 Roberts, Cecil. *One Small Candle.* Macmillan, 1970. Gr. 9- . Paul Korwienski, a Polish pianist, marries an American movie star just before the Second World War. (Music; Romance)

521 Sendak, Philip. *In Grandpa's House.* Harper, 1985. Gr. 3-4. A father, a Jewish immigrant, wishes to share his values with his son. His son is the famous illustrator/author Maurice Sendak. (Values; Biography, Fictionalized)

522 Waterton, Betty. *Petranella.* Vanguard, 1980. Gr. K-3. Petranella's grandmother gives her a bag of seeds to plant at their new home in America. She loses the seeds when their oxcart slips on the way to their home. She later finds the seeds have sprouted by the road. (Girls, Preteen; Plants)

523 Wisniowski, Sygurd. *Ameryka 100 Years Old.* Cherry Hill, 1972. Gr. 9- . Stories of love, adjustment, loneliness and life on the American frontier as Poles settle the American West. (West, American; Lonesomeness)

PORTUGUESE

See also HISPANIC

524 Foltz, Mary Jane. *Nicolau's Prize.* McGraw, 1967. Gr. 4-5. Nicolau's father is a whaler and Nicolau has the whale oil smell about him. He is made fun of at school. When the school takes a field trip to the whaling business they learn to respect Nicolau's father's trade. (Working World; Boys, Pre-teen)

525 Newman, Shirlee P. *Shipwrecked Dog.* Bobbs, 1963. Gr. 4-6. Carlos was lonely in America and longed to return to Portugal. When he acquired a homeless puppy it changed his feeling about home. (Dogs; Lonesomeness)

526 Patton, Willoughby. *Manuel's Discovery.* McKay, 1970. Gr. 4-6. Wanting to be considered a real Bermudian, a boy, 13, is resentful of his family's Portuguese background until he goes with his grandfather to visit the Azores. (Cultural Differences; Island Life)

PRUSSIAN

See GERMAN

PUERTO RICAN

See also WEST INDIAN

527 Barth, Edna. *Day Luis Was Lost.* Little, 1971. Gr. 2-4. Forced to detour on his way to school, Luis ends up in a police station. (Boys, Pre-teen; Adventure)

528 Belpre, Pura. *Santiago.* Warne, 1969. Gr. 1-4. A Puerto Rican boy tries to adjust to his new home in New York City. He tells about his pretty pet hen, Selina, he left behind. (Poultry)

529 Bethancourt, T.E. *New York City, Too Far from Tampa Blues*. Holiday, 1975. Gr. 7-9. Tom has adjustments to make as he tries for a corner shoeshine job. His friend, Aurelio, and he form a group and perform for money. They get so good they make a recording. (Music; Urban Life)

530 Bethancourt, T.E. *Where the Deer and the Cantaloupe Play*. Oak Tree, 1981. Gr. 7-9. Teddy dreams of being a cowboy like his great-grandfather. He learns all the techniques. He goes to California and becomes an expert rodeo entertainer. (Boys, Mature; Gangs; West, American)

531 Binzen, William. *Miguel's Mountain*. Coward, 1969. Gr. K-3. Miguel's mountain is a pile of dirt heaped up by construction men working in the area. Because the children are used to playing on concrete in the ghetto, this pile of dirt is a treat. (Boys, Pre-teen; Play)

532 Binzen, William. *Carmen*. Coward, 1970. Gr. K-3. Carmen makes her first friend in New York when she waves at another girl at the window across the street from her apartment. They are both waiting for the rain to stop. (Urban Life; Friendship Among Girls)

533 Blue, Rose. *I Am Here: Yo Estoy Aqui*. Watts, 1971. Gr. K-2. On her first day in kindergarten, a little Puerto Rican girl feels lost and unhappy. Then she learns a few English words and feels better. (School; Language Differences)

534 Bonham, Frank. *Mystery of the Fat Cat*. Dutton, 1968. Gr. 4-6. A mystery centering around a large inheritance, with a group of Puerto Ricans as detectives. (Mystery)

535 Bouchard, Lois. *Boy Who Wouldn't Talk*. Doubleday, 1969. Gr. 4-5. Carlos' family moved from Puerto Rico. He can't easily learn the English language and so gives up talking at all. He meets Ricky, who is blind and needs directions; Carlos must talk. (Boys, Teen; Blindness; Language Differences)

536 Bourne, M. *Emilio's Summer Day*. Harper, 1966. Gr. K-3. A boy looks for something to do on a hot afternoon and finds it when the street washer's truck swishes by. (Boys, Pre-teen; Play)

537 Brenner, Barbara. *Barto Takes the Subway*. Knopf, 1961. Gr. 3-5. Barto and his sister take a trip on the New York Subway. (Urban Life; Brothers & Sisters)

538 Burchard, Peter. *Chito*. Coward, 1969. Gr. 3-4. Chito is a new arrival in Spanish Harlem; he experiences fears, doubts and uneasiness. He is worried about being accepted in this alien neighborhood. His new friend, Juan, helps him adjust. (Self-Esteem; Fears)

539 Burchardt, Nellie. *Surprise for Carlotta*. Watts, 1971. Gr. 3-5. A family story of Puerto Ricans living in New York. Carlotta, eight, experiences all the different changes. (Girls, Pre-teen; Family)

540 Campion, Wardi. *Casa Means Home*. Holt, 1976. Gr. 4–6. Lorenzo is a Puerto Rican living in New York. He has problems in school, is afraid of many things and can't have a wanted pet. He goes back to Puerto Rico for the summer, works hard but returns to New York. (Urban Life)

541 Christopher, Matt. *Baseball Flyhawk*. Little, 1963. Gr. 4–6. Chico, Buddy and String play baseball. There are competition, friendship and life saving rescues. Chico learns that he can be a friend and team member even though he is Puerto Rican. (Sports/Baseball)

542 Cofer, Judith. *Line of the Sun*. Univ. of Georgia Press, 1989. Gr. 9– . Guzman was born in Puerto Rico but lives in New York City. He is misunderstood and therefore has as many tragedies as adventures. The story contrasts life in rural Puerto Rico and urban New York City. (Cultural Differences; Rural Life; Urban Life)

543 Cofer, Judith. *Silent Dancing*. Arte Publico, 1990. Gr. 9– . Short stories for girls about the trials and anxieties of growing up in America with a Puerto Rican background. (Short Stories; Girls, Teen)

544 Colman, Hila. *Girl from Puerto Rico*. Morrow, 1961. Gr. 7– . The conflict that a girl experiences when she moves to New York City from Puerto Rico. (Girls, Teen; Prejudice)

545 Crane, Caroline. *Don't Look at Me That Way*. Random, 1970. Gr. 5–8. Rosa is the oldest of seven children. They have no father and grow up under difficult conditions. (Family)

546 Danska, Herbert. *Street Kids*. Knopf, 1970. Gr. 7–9. A watchman at a construction site where a strike is going on befriends some "street kids." They plant a flower garden which grows, blooms and covers some of the unfinished building. (Working World; Friendship)

547 Figueroa, John. *Antonio's World*. Random, 1970. Gr. 3–5. A Puerto Rican boy, 13, gets a job and is then fired; he tries kite flying in the city. (Working World; Kites)

548 Figueroa, Pablo. *Enrique*. Random, 1970. Gr. 5–8. Enrique is warned about a murderer in his new neighborhood in the ghetto of New York. An exciting story revealing family life and culture. (Mystery; Family)

549 Fleischman, H. Samuel. *Gang Girl*. Doubleday, 1967. Gr. 5–8. Maria, 14, lives in New York City. She is rejected by her stepfather and ignored by her mother. She joins a gang called "Spanish Ladies." She gets into trouble but changes for the better. (Girls, Teen; Gangs)

550 Garcia, Richard. *My Aunt Otilia's Spirits*. Children's, 1987. Gr. 4–6. When Aunt Otilia comes to visit she brings some unpleasant ghosts to scare her nephew. But he, in turn, really scares her. (Ghosts; Family)

551 Gault, William. *Backfield Challenge.* Dutton, 1967. Gr. 7-9. Johnny, a Puerto Rican, attends a white middle class school. He is resented even though he plays football for the school team. Link is a black schoolmate and gets more criticism. (Sports/Football; Prejudice)

552 Gonzalez, Gloria. *Gaucho.* Knopf, 1977. Gr. 4-7. Gaucho, 12, lives on welfare in New York City with his mother. He wants to go back to Puerto Rico and tries to raise money to do so. (Urban Life; Moneymaking; Mothers & Sons)

553 Gray, Genevieve. *Dark Side of Nowhere.* EMC, 1977. Gr. 4-6. A story of Puerto Ricans during the blackout of November 9, 1965, in New York City. A robbery was attempted but stopped by the men and a baby was born. (Family; Community Life)

554 Greene, Roberta. *Two and Me Makes Three.* Coward, 1970. Gr. K-2. After a fight it takes three friends a week to apologize to each other. (Friendship; Values)

555 Hall, Lynn. *Danza.* Scribner, 1981. Gr. 5-8. Paulo loves Danza, one of his grandfather's horses that his grandfather thinks is worthless, a Paso Fino. Danza gets ill but Paulo sticks by him and eventually shows the worth of the horse. (Horses, Trained)

556 Hearn, Emily. *Around Another Corner.* Garrard, 1971. Gr. K-3. Peppino, a young boy, offers to help the mailman, the painter, the policeman and others. But he is too small to help. Then he sees Joe, who is picking up litter. He can do that and Joe needs help. (Boys, Pre-teen; Values)

557 Heuman, William. *City High Champion.* Dodd, 1969. Gr. 5-8. Tex is the star basketball player and resents the Puerto Rican, Pedro, who plays on the team. (Sports/Basketball; School)

558 Heuman, William. *Little League Hotshots.* Dodd, 1972. Gr. 4-6. Newly arrived from Puerto Rico, a young boy is lonely until he becomes a member of a Little League team. (Sports/Baseball; Lonesomeness)

559 Hurwitz, Johanna. *Class President.* Morrow, 1990. Gr. 4-6. Julio has thoughts of being a school leader but instead helps another candidate win the nomination. (School; Leadership)

560 Keats, Ezra. *My Dog Is Lost!* Crowell, 1960. Gr. K-2. A Spanish-speaking bank teller and a group of Harlem children join Juanito, newly arrived in New York from Puerto Rico, in search of his lost dog, Pepito. (Dogs; Community Life)

561 Kesselman, Wendy. *Angelita.* Hill & Wang, 1970. Gr. K-3. Angelita moves to New York, where she feels caged in, and then she finds her old rag doll. One day she loses it. (Actually it is taken by some bully boys.) Julio hides it but he repents and returns it to her as a friend. (Urban Life; Friendship)

562 Kuklin, Susan. *How My Family Lives in America.* Bradbury, 1992. Gr. K-3. A family that live in America but follow traditions of their homeland; they choose to accept American traditions also. They like baseball, American food and music; they learn the language and games, etc. (Family; Cultural Differences)

563 Levoy, Myron. *Shadow Like a Leopard.* Harper, 1981. Gr. 7-9. Ramon carries a knife and wants to be a gang member. He wants to prove himself but finds a kindred spirit in the old artist and starts a new life. (Gangs; Arts & Artists)

564 Lewiton, Mina. *Candita's Choice.* Harper, 1959. Gr. 3-6. Candita, 11, refused to speak until she could speak English properly. She wanted her teacher to be proud of her. She wanted to stop missing her home and friends in Puerto Rico. (School)

565 Lewiton, Mina. *That Bad Carlos.* Harper, 1964. Gr. 4-6. The story of how Carlos came to understand borrowing and stealing and the difference between right and wrong. (Values)

566 Lexau, Joan. *Jose's Christmas Secret.* Dial, 1963. Gr. 3-5. A ten-year-old boy living in New York is acting head of household and is determined to buy a warm blanket for his mother. (Holidays; Mothers & Sons)

567 Lexau, Joan. *Maria.* Dial, 1964. Gr. K-2. Maria was disappointed because she could not play with her valuable doll; however, her family did get a doll she could hold and cuddle. (Dolls)

568 McCabe, Inger. *Week in Henry's World.* Macmillan, 1971. Gr. K-3. Henry lives in "El Barrio" in New York City. There are drug users and drunks there; there are poverty and broken families; there is also hope for those who play and work together. (Family; Poverty)

569 Mann, Peggy. *Clubhouse.* Coward, 1969. Gr. 4-5. Carlos, nine, takes charge of transforming his community into a better place. He and his cousin, Jose, meet in Carlos' clubhouse, a burned out building. (Boys, Pre-teen; Community Life)

570 Mann, Peggy. *How Juan Got Home.* Coward, 1972. Gr. 4-6. Juan comes to live with his godfather in New York. He doesn't know the language and has trouble making friends. But he meets a friend with whom he plays ball; he becomes a hero. Home has a double meaning here. (Boys, Teen; Language Differences; Sports/Baseball)

571 Mann, Peggy. *Street of the Flower Boxes.* Coward, 1966. Gr. 4-6. Carlos and a group of youngsters from West 94th Street set about beautifying their part of the block by selling window boxes. (Urban Life; Community Life)

572 Mann, Peggy. *When Carlos Closed the Street.* Coward, 1969. Gr. 3-6. Carlos' gang and Jimmy's gang had territorial lines that nobody crossed. One day Carlos crossed it and was challenged to a game of stickball. They closed off the street and caused a traffic tie-up. (Gangs; Humorous)

573   Martel, Cruz. *Yagua Days.* Dial, 1976. Gr. K-3. Adan visits relatives in Puerto Rico and finds the meaning of yagua days: belly flopping on the edge of the river on a banana leaf on rainy days. (Family)

574   Means, Florence. *Us Maltbys.* Houghton, 1966. Gr. 7-9. M.J. and Sylly's parents take in five foster children, all girls, some of whom are Mexican or Puerto Rican. The town is upset and against this; but the girls are nice and it works out well. (Foster Care; Prejudice)

575   Melendez, Carmello. *Long Time Growing.* Children's, 1970. Gr. 7- . Carmello and his mother search for his father. They find him in Indiana but life is still hard. Carmello studies to become an X-ray technician in spite of language and financial problems. (Boys, Teen; Careers)

576   Mohr, Nicholasa. *El Bronx Remembered.* Harper, 1975. Gr. 9- . The sights, sounds and people of the Puerto Rican barrio in New York City in the late '40s and early '50s. Family life, the death of a baby, pregnancy and growing up are included. (Family; Short Stories)

577   Mohr, Nicholasa. *Felita.* Dial, 1979. Gr. 4-6. Felita is Puerto Rican and has difficulty making friends in her new neighborhood. The Maldonado family move back to their old neighborhood when their new neighbors get really nasty. (Prejudice; Community Life)

578   Mohr, Nicholasa. *Going Home.* Dial, 1986. Gr. 5-8. Felita is going to spend the summer in Puerto Rico. There are restrictions for young girls both at home and in Puerto Rico, but Felita finds friends in both places and matures in the process. (Girls, Teen; Family)

579   Mohr, Nicholasa. *In Nueva York.* Arte Publico, 1988. Gr. 7-9. Short stories depicting the lives of Puerto Ricans living in New York's poverty stricken East Side. (Poverty; Short Stories)

580   Mohr, Nicholasa. *Nilda.* Harper, 1973. Gr. 7-9. The tenement stoops of El Barrio are the home grounds of Nilda, age 10. She lives there during the Second World War and suffers from being a Puerto Rican in New York at this time. (Prejudice; Poverty)

581   Molnar, Joe. *Elizabeth.* Watts, 1974. Gr. K-2. A Puerto Rican girl living in East Harlem describes her family, social and school life and her impressions of Puerto Rico after a visit there. (Girls, Teen; Family; School)

582   Moore, Ruth. *Tomas and the Talking Birds.* Herald, 1979. Gr. 4-6. Tomas, 10, is lonely at school because of a language barrier. He is laughed at when he talks about Puerto Rico. He is told to try

hard to learn to speak English. (Boys, Pre-teen; Language Differences)

583 Prieto, Mariana. *Tomato Boy*. Day, 1967. Gr. 3–5. Davey delivers tomatoes from door to door. His friend is Paco, a Puerto Rican. Davey needs the money for a shirt, Paco needs money for shoes. They need these items for roles in a school show. (Friendship; Loyalty)

584 Reit, Seymour. *Dear Uncle Carlos*. McGraw, 1969. Gr. K–3. Wanda writes a birthday note to her Uncle Carlos, who lives in Puerto Rico. Her mother and father help. (Family; Girls, Pre-teen; Birthdays)

585 Rivera, Edward. *Family Installments*. Morrow, 1982. Gr. 9– . A fictional biography of a Puerto Rican boy growing up in New York. There is a great deal of humor and pride in the telling. (Boys, Teen; Biography, Fictionalized; Humorous)

586 Sachs, Marilyn. *Truth About Mary Rose*. Doubleday, 1973. Gr. 4–7. Mary Rose, Veronica's daughter, investigates the truth about her late aunt, Mary Rose, who was her namesake. Was she the heroine who saved tenants in an apartment fire, or not? (Girls, Pre-teen; Family)

587 Shearer, J. *Little Man in the Family*. Delacorte, 1972. Gr. 3–4. An inner city Puerto Rican boy and an upper middle class white boy talk about their daily life and their ambitions for the future. (Boys, Teen; Daily Life)

588 Shotwell, Louisa. *Adam Bookout*. Viking, 1967. Gr. 5–8. Adam, who is white, makes friends with a black, a Jew and a Puerto Rican in his Brooklyn neighborhood. Together they solve a neighborhood crime of dog stealing. (Boys, Pre-teen; Community Life; Crime)

589 Shotwell, Louisa. *Magdalena*. Viking, 1971. Gr. 4–6. Magdalena wants her hair cut so she will look more American. Her traditional grandmother is against it, but Magdalena cuts it anyway. Magdalena, her friend Spook and her grandmother accept the change. (Girls, Teen; Generation Gap)

590 Shyer, Marlene. *Tino*. Random, 1969. Gr. 4–6. Tino's uncle has a motto, "Fun first, worry later." Tino gets an egg, from which hatches a chicken that he raises in his apartment. (Humorous; Poultry)

591 Solbert, Ronnie. *I Wrote My Name on the Wall*. Little, 1971. Gr. K–2. Photographs and brief text record the limited world of ghetto children who have never traveled beyond their neighborhoods. A description of games played in the streets by immigrant children. (Music; Community Life; Games)

592 Sonneborn, Ruth. *Friday Night Is Papa Night*. Viking, 1970. Gr. K–2. Papa's work takes him away from home through the week, but he comes home with money and gifts each Friday night. (Family; Gifts; Working World)

593 Sonneborn, Ruth. *Lollipop Party.* Viking, 1967. Gr. K-2. Tomas stays alone in the apartment for the first time waiting for his mother to get home; and the long and scary wait turns into a lollipop party. (Urban Life)

594 Sonneborn, Ruth. *Seven in Bed.* Viking, 1968. Gr. K-2. Papa meets the plane at the airport but there are seven ninos and Mama — four more than he expected. Where will everyone sleep? (Family)

595 Speevack, Yetta. *Spider Plant.* Atheneum, 1965. Gr. 4-6. Carmen is from Puerto Rico and makes friends in her neighborhood. But the building in which she lives is to come down, and she must move again to a new place. Her spider plant is a symbol of her ability to accept change. (Self-Esteem; Community Life)

596 Talbot, Charlene. *Tomas Takes Charge.* Lothrop, 1966. Gr. 3-5. When his father disappears, a Puerto Rican boy and his sister find a place to live and a way to support themselves. (Brothers & Sisters)

597 Talbot, Toby. *My House Is Your House.* Cowles, 1970. Gr. K-3. Juana, 10, is desolate when her old block is condemned to make way for new housing; she discovers that home means more than a house. (Urban Life; Community Life)

598 Thaler, Susan. *Rosaria.* McKay, 1967. Gr. 4-6. A bright and sensitive 15-year-old Puerto Rican girl living in New York has the ability to rise above her surroundings, but she loses all faith and hope when her father deserts the family. (Delinquency; Girls, Teen)

599 Thomas, Dawn. *Mira! Mira!* Lippincott, 1970. Gr. K-3. Ramon has just arrived in New York City and is excited about seeing snow. His mother goes to buy him winter clothes, but he plays in the snow without proper clothing and gets sick. (Boys, Pre-teen; Family; Play)

600 Thomas Dawn. *Pablito's New Feet.* Lippincott, 1973. Gr. 1-3. With the help of doctors and his large family, a young Puerto Rican boy afflicted with polio learns to walk. (Physically Handicapped; Family; Health & Medicine)

601 Weiner, Sandra. *They Call Me Jack.* Pantheon, 1973. Gr. 4-6. Jacinto, 10, talks about his home and family as he compares houses, food, school, environment and family life in New York with these things in Puerto Rico. (Boys, Preteen; Cultural Differences; Daily Life)

RUSSIAN

602 Angell, Judie. *One-Way to Ansonia.* Bradbury, 1985. Gr. 7- . Rose must get away from her cruel employer and find safety. She takes her three dollars and buys a ticket to Ansonia Station. The story tells of her life as an immigrant in the late 1800s. (Historical Fiction)

603 Berman, Chaim. *Patriarch.* St. Martin's, 1981. Gr. 9- . A realistic story of a Russian Jewish family who came to America in the early 1900s. (Family)

604 Bernstein, Joanne. *Dmitry: A Young Soviet Immigrant.* Houghton, 1981. Gr. 5-8. A story of a boy's life in America after he and his family arrived from Russia. (Family; Boys, Teen)

605 Betancourt, Jeanne. *Home Sweet Home.* Bantam, 1988. Gr. 7-9. Tracy makes friends with Anya, an exchange student from Russia. Anya gives her views of American boys, schools, and freedom. Tracy sees her own country through different eyes. (Girls, Teen; Cultural Differences)

606 Blue, Rose. *Cold Rain on the Water.* McGraw, 1979. Gr. 7-9. Grandpa, Mama, Papa, Natasha and Alex leave Russia for America. Natasha attends school, Alex makes friends and Grandpa loves it all. Only Papa is unhappy; he must take a dangerous second job. (Family; Working World)

607 Bullard, Arthur. *Comrade Yetta.* Gregg, 1969. Gr. 9- . Yetta comes to America from Russia. She works in a sweat shop with other immigrant children. She eventually becomes a union organizer. (Working World; Women's Rights)

608 Cahan, Abraham. *Rise of David Levinsky.* Harper, 1917. Gr. 8- . David comes to New York in 1885 and becomes a pushcart peddler. He then gets into the garment trade and is successful but wonders if he should not have lived his life differently. (Working World; Careers)

609 Caseley, Judith. *Apple Pie and Onions.* Greenwillow, 1987. Gr. K-2. Rebecca loves to hear her grandmother's stories about how she came to America, even though they do embarrass her sometimes. (Grandparents)

610 Chec, John. *My Grandmother's Journey.* Bradbury, 1991. Gr. K-2. Korie's grandmother tells of her journey out of Russia, her survival and her trip to America. (Grandparents)

611 Christopher, Matt. *Look Who's Playing First Base.* Little, 1971. Gr. 4-6. Yuri is new to both America and baseball. He nearly loses Mike as a friend and his spot on the baseball team, but he then wins a game and becomes a great player. (Sports/Baseball)

612 Clark, Margery. *Poppy Seed Cakes.* Doubleday, 1927. Gr. 2-4. A story of Andrewshek and his family showing happy times and closeness of family. Andrewshek's Aunt Katushka comes to visit and brings gifts, among them poppy seeds to put on the cakes she'll bake. (Family; Boys, Pre-teen; Food)

613 Cohen, Barbara. *Gooseberries to Oranges.* Lothrop, 1982. Gr. 1-3. When Eastern Europe is devastated by cholera and persecution, Fanny, eight, goes to the United States and is reunited with her father. She tastes her first orange and finds a new home. (Fathers & Daughters)

614 Cohen, Barbara. *Molly's Pilgrim.* Lothrop, 1983. Gr. 2-5. Molly and her family just arrived from Russia and she was being teased about her clothes and accent. She brought to school, for an assigned project, a clothespin doll of a "pilgrim," a peasant. (School; Jews)

615 Colman, Hila. *Rachel's Legacy.* Crown, 1979. Gr. 7-9. Ellie's mother, Rachel, tells of life in New York for Jewish immigrants during the Depression. Her two sisters took different paths to success. Ellie is like her mother. (Jews; Sisters; Depression Era)

616 Crayder, Dorothy. *Joker and the Swan.* Harper, 1981. Gr. 4-6. Zoe, 11, wants to be a ballerina. She and Tavia are in the same class taught by Madame Polinki. Tavia is singled out for awards and Zoe is terribly jealous. (Ballet; Girls, Teen; Jealousy)

617 Curley, Daniel. *Hilarion.* Houghton, 1979. Gr. 4-6. Four tradesmen are in America looking for work but are discouraged. When Hilarion from the Old Country joins them, he brings encouragement. (Urban Life; Working World)

618 Farrar, Susan C. *Samantha on Stage.* Dial, 1979. Gr. 5-8. Samantha meets a Russian girl who studied at the Bolshoi. At first she is competitive but she learns from the talented Lizinka and they both have success. (Ballet; Friendship Among Girls)

619 Fine, Anne. *Granny Project.* Farrar, 1983. Gr. 5-8. Ivan, Sophie, Tanya and Nicholas work on a project to keep Granny from going into a nursing home. (Grandparents; Brothers & Sisters)

620 Forman, Marcey. *Russian in the Attic.* Winston-Derek, 1988. Gr. 4-6. Mikhail, 12, doesn't want to return to Russia when his embassy father is ordered to return. He runs away and tries to hide. He expresses reasons for his love of America and fear of Russia. (Boys, Pre-teen; Runaways)

621 Gelfand, Marilyn. *My Great-Grandpa Joe.* Macmillan, 1986. Gr. K-3. Debbie, eight, loves to visit her great-grandparents. She learns of Joe and Sara's life together. Sara was a good cook and mother. She also worked outside the home, joined a union, and was politically involved. (Grandparents; Women)

622 Geras, Adele. *Voyage.* Atheneum, 1983. Gr. 7- . Minna, Golda and Rachel are sisters aboard the SS *Danzig* headed for America in 1904. Minna is the strength for her mother and brother, Golda is going to see her husband and Rachel, not as strong as Minna, fears the future. (Family; Jews)

623 Harvey, Brett. *Immigrant Girl.* Holiday House, 1987. Gr. 2-4. Becky, ten, and her family came from Russia. They find New York City in 1910 very exciting.

They live over the family grocery store and Becky helps with chores, cares for the baby and shops. (Jews; Daily Life)

624 Heller, Linda. *Castle on Hester Street.* Jewish Pub. Society, 1932. Gr. K–2. Julie's grandfather tells fantastic stories about his arrival in America. Her grandmother explains what really happened: a crowded boat, a small apartment, selling from a pushcart, working night and day. (Humorous; Values)

625 Lasky, Kathryn. *Night Journey.* Warne, 1981. Gr. 7– . Rachel tells the story of the escape of her family from the persecutions of Tsarist Russia. She reveals the life of her great-grandmother in the telling. (Jews; Family; Grandparents)

626 Lehrman, Robert. *Store That Mama Built.* Macmillan, 1992. Gr. 4–6. Birdie, 12, and her siblings help their mother run the family store. They lost their father and are trying to pick up where he left off: to succeed in America. (Working World; Family)

627 Lelchuk, Alan. *On Home Ground.* Harcourt, 1987. Gr. 5–8. A baseball story that raises social issues. Aaron loves baseball and neglects other things in favor of the game. His father is a strict Socialist. Aaron and his father find they have to make hard choices. (Sports/Baseball; Decisions; Fathers & Sons)

628 McLerran, Alice. *Secrets.* Lothrop, 1990. Gr. 4–6. Mark makes friends with Olga Zhavoronkov; his sister, Meg, makes friends with Natasha. They share stories about each other's country and teach each other their language. (Friendship; Cultural Traits)

629 Maguire, Gregory. *Daughter of the Moon.* Farrar, 1980. Gr. 4–5. Modest left Russia and his girlfriend because of terror. For 60 years he remains faithful to her even though they have lost touch with one another. Erika, 12, helps to reunite them. (Romance; Loyalty)

630 Moskin, Marietta. *Waiting for Mama.* Coward, 1975. Gr. 4–6. Would Becky's mother like America as she now does? She remembers how she, Rachel and Jake hated it at first. (Jews; Mothers)

631 Nathan, Dorothy. *Shy One.* Random, 1966. Gr. 4–6. Dorothy is the "Shy One." She is in the fifth grade and afraid of most things. Her grandmother and Uncle Max are coming from Russia to visit, so she forces herself to become outgoing and involved. (Family; Self-Esteem)

632 Nixon, Joan. *Land of Hope.* Bantam, 1992. Gr. 5–8. Rebekah leaves Russia and flees to New York City. A rendering of life for immigrants in the early 1990s. (Urban Life)

633 Papashvily, George. *Home and Home Again.* Harper, 1973. Gr. 7– . Papashvily and his wife are immigrants from Russia. They live a good life. Fifty years later he returns to the city of his birth. (Family)

634 Polacco, Patricia. *Keeping Quilt*. Simon & Schuster, 1988. Gr. K-2. Four generations of Jewish immigrants are linked by a homemade quilt. (Jews; Family)

635 Polacco, Patricia. *Thunder Cake*. Philomel, 1990. Gr. K-3. A Russian grandmother on a Michigan farm helps her grandchild cope with thunderstorms. She gathers all the needed ingredients as the storm approaches and makes the cake as the thunder claps. (Fear; Grandparents; Weather)

636 Polacco, Patricia. *Uncle Vova's Tree*. Philomel, 1989. Gr. K-3. The whole family: grandparents, aunts and uncles, parents, sisters, brothers, children and grandchildren get together at Uncle Vova's at Christmastime and celebrate in a traditional manner. (Holidays; Family)

637 Roseman, Kenneth. *Melting Pot*. Union of American Hebrew Congregations, 1984. Gr. 5-8. A young Jewish immigrant in New York must make serious decisions about his life in a new country. (Jews; Decisions)

638 Sachs, Marilyn. *Call Me Ruth*. Doubleday, 1982. Gr. 5-8. Ruth is an immigrant who is at odds with her mother because of the different opinion of whether to keep the old traditions or accept the new and different. (Working World; Mothers & Daughters)

639 Sherman, Eileen. *Independence Avenue*. Jewish Pub. Society, 1990. Gr. 7-9. Elias, 14, arrives alone in Kansas City. He finds a job and new friends but gets bad news about his family back in Russia. (Boys, Teen; Family)

640 Shiefman, Vicky. *Goodbye to the Trees*. Macmillan, 1993. Gr. 8- . Fagel, 13, is excited about her new life in America, but she thinks about the family she left behind. (Girls, Teen; Family)

641 Tobenkin, Elias. *Witte Arrives*. Gregg, 1969. Gr. 9- . Emil, a Jew, emigrated from Russia. He adjusts and works his way through college. He becomes a reporter in Chicago, marries a Gentile girl and must again adjust to a non-Jewish community. (Jews; College; Journalism)

642 Tolstoy, Leo. *Lion and the Puppy*. Holt, 1988. Gr. 3-5. A collection of stories written for peasant children learning to read at the school where Tolstoy taught in 1849. Stories with moral values, wonders of nature and everyday wisdom. (Short Stories; Values)

643 Vineberg, Ethel. *Grandmother Came from Dworitz*. Tundra, 1969. Gr. 5-8. A story about the life of Russian Jews. They were restricted to living in a shtetl where the synagogue was the center of life. Many of them immigrated to America and Canada. (Jews)

644 Williams, Jeanne. *Winter Wheat*. Putnam, 1975. Gr. 5-8. Cobie tells of her family's journey from Russia to the plains of Kansas. They endure grasshoppers, prairie fires and rabid animals, but they make friends and learn to love the land. (West, American)

645 Yezierska, Anzia. *How I Found America*. Brazeller, 1991. Gr. 9- . Short stories about a young Russian Jewish woman in New York in the 1920s and 1930s. (Short Stories; Jews)

SCOTTISH

646 Buchan, Bryan. *Copper Sunrise*. Scholastic, 1972. Gr. 4-6. A Scottish settler and an Indian become friends. They discover the differences in their culture; they feel ill at ease but overcome this as they discover common interests. (Cultural Difference; Friendship; Native American)

647 Capron, Louis. *Red War Pole*. Bobbs, 1963. Gr. 5-8. Allan, of Scottish descent, lives in Florida and wants to make peace between his family and the Seminole Indians in the 1830s. (Seminole)

648 Clarke, Mary. *Iron Peacock*. Viking, 1966. Gr. 7-9. Ross McCrae, a Scottish prisoner and Joanna, who is 16 and fleeing from Cromwell's England, try to build a new life in early America. They are indentured to the Iron Master. (Colonial America; Slavery)

649 De Mejo, Oscar. *Forty-Niners*. Harper, 1985. Gr. K-3. A Scottish immigrant, Homer, has many adventures in America, including mining for gold and dealing with an evil gold prospector. (Adventure; Mines & Mining)

650 Harris, Christie. *Forbidden Frontier*. Atheneum, 1968. Gr. 7-9. Alison is the daughter of a Scottish trader and a Haida Indian. Megan is the daughter of Irish immigrants. Both girls are rebels, but they want to see Indian justice. (Girls, Teen; Justice)

651 Hays, Wilma. *Highland Halloween*. Coward, 1962. Gr. 4-5. Robbie and Archie go out on Halloween night to a haunted house. (Holidays)

652 Lofts, Nora. *Blossom like a Rose*. Knopf, 1973. Gr. 9- . A young Scottish boy is crippled and bitter about it. He is an immigrant in America and wealthy. (Physically Handicapped; Romance)

653 Watson, Sally. *Hornet's Nest*. Holt, 1968. Gr. 8- . A story of the Scots who were being mistreated by the British after the 1745 uprising. They later left for America and settled in Williamsburg in 1775. (Colonial America)

654 Weller, Frances. *Boat Song*. Macmillan, 1987. Gr. 5-8. Jonno feels misunderstood and unaccepted. On summer vacation he meets Rob, a Scottish piper who becomes a father figure. (Fathers; Music; Self-Esteem)

SENEGALESE

655 Kuklin, Susan. *How My Family Lives in America*. Bradbury,

1992. Gr. K-3. A family that live in America but follow traditions of their homeland; they choose to accept American traditions also. They like baseball, American food and music; they learn the language and games. (Family; Cultural Differences)

656 O'Dell, Scott. *My Name Is Not Angelica.* Houghton, 1989. Gr. 5-8. A story of the slave rebellion of 1773 on the island of St. John as told by Raisha, a Senegalese girl, who is a body slave of a planter's wife. (Slavery)

SPANISH

See also HISPANIC

657 Clark, Ann Nolan. *Year Walk.* Viking, 1975. Gr. 5-8. Kepa, a 15-year-old boy, moves from being a Basque sheepherder to an Idaho homesteader in the early 1990s. (Frontier Life)

658 Forbes, Harrie. *Mission Tales in the Days of the Dons.* Books for Libraries, 1970. Gr. 9- . Short stories about Spanish America in the early days of settlement. (Short Stories)

659 McGiffin, Lee. *Riders of Enchanted Valley.* Dutton, 1966. Gr. 7- . Luke, 15, goes to live with his brother in California. His brother is married to a Spanish girl. Their home life is different and exciting. (Brothers; Rural Life)

660 Price, Eugenia. *Don Juan McQueen.* Lippincott, 1974. Gr. 7- . Don Juan is aide to the governor of Florida under Spanish rule. A picture of the romantic and tragic life in St. Augustine, Florida. (Description)

SWEDISH

661 Budd, Lillian. *April Harvest.* Duell, 1959. Gr. 8- . Sigrid, 17, is orphaned when her father dies but is determined to be self-sufficient. She has many happy and unhappy experiences as she unravels her father's diary and wins a writing contest. (Prejudice; Writing; Girls, Mature)

662 Christgau, Alice. *Runaway to Glory.* Scott, 1965. Gr. 4-6. Rueben is friendly with his stepgrandpa. They help capture some thieves and become heroes. (Family; Crime)

663 Ericson, Stig. *Dan Henry in the Wild West.* Delacorte, 1976. Gr. 7-9. Dan arrives in Minnesota in 1870 with his friend Martin. Martin is shot by the James Gang and Dan moves west and joins the United States cavalry. (Frontier Life; Friendship Among Boys)

664 Johnson, Lois W. *Trouble at Wild River.* Bethany, 1991. Gr. 5-8. Kate and her friends see a timber swindler while visiting Running Deer. They all suspect Kate's uncle may be involved. He just recently arrived from Sweden. (Mystery; Working World)

665 Lindquist, Jennie. *Crystal Tree.* Harper, 1966. Gr. 9- . Nancy and her friends wait for a house to open that has been boarded up for thirty years. A good Swedish-American family story. (Family)

666 Lindquist, Jennie. *Golden Name Day.* Harper, 1955. Gr. 4-6. Nancy's life is parties and fun. A name day must be found for her. It is a problem because she is not in the Swedish almanac, but the search goes on. (Girls, Teen; Names)

667 Lindquist, Jennie. *Little Silver House.* Harper, 1960. Gr. 4-6. Nancy is back home with her mother and grows up in the early 1900s in New England. But she is surrounded by customs and traditions of Scandinavia. (Mothers & Daughter; Cultural Traits; Lifestyle)

668 Moberg, Vilhelm. *Emigrants.* Simon & Schuster, 1971. Gr. 7- . A family immigrate to New York and talk about why they made the move. This is book one of a trilogy. (Family)

669 Moberg, Vilhelm. *Unto a Good Land.* Simon & Schuster, 1954. Gr. 8- . Karl and his family came to America in 1850. They move from New York to Minnesota using many different modes of transportation. Once there, Karl fells trees and builds a home. This is book two of a trilogy. (Cultural Traits; Family)

670 Norris, Gunella. *Feast of Light.* Knopf, 1967. Gr. 4-6. Ulla, 10, feels the differences between herself and her classmates. She has a language problem and trouble at school causes trouble at home. (Girls, Pre-teen; School)

671 Sandin, Joan. *Long Way to a New Land.* Harper, 1981. Gr. 1-3. A Swedish family leave their drought-stricken land and immigrate to the United States. Their trip is harrowing but there is hope in America. (Family)

672 Sandin, Joan. *Long Way Westward.* Harper, 1989. Gr. 1-3. A family of immigrants from Sweden, with two brothers, move from New York to Minnesota. (Family; Brothers)

673 Shaw, Janet. *Changes for Kirsten.* Pleasant, 1988. Gr. 4-5. Kirsten spends her first winter in Minnesota. She helps her brother set his traps and helps her family move into a new house. (Frontier Life; Brothers & Sisters)

674 Shaw, Janet. *Happy Birthday, Kirsten!* Pleasant, 1987. Gr. 3-4. Kirsten lives in Minnesota in 1854. It is her birthday and she expects no gifts. What she does want, and gets, is a day off from her everyday chores. (Frontier Life; Birthday)

675 Shaw, Janet. *Kirsten Learns a Lesson.* Pleasant, 1986. Gr. 4-5. Kirsten is from Sweden. She finds American schools strange, but she makes a secret friend with an Indian girl and learns to endure. (Frontier Life; Friendship Among Girls)

676 Shaw, Janet. *Kirsten Saves the Day.* Pleasant, 1988. Gr. 4-5.

Kirsten, ten, finds a beehive full of honey. She almost has a tragedy as she tries to harvest the honey herself. (Frontier Life; Girls, Pre-teen)

677 Shaw, Janet. *Kirsten's Surprise*. Pleasant, 1986. Gr. 4-5. Kirsten and her family, from Sweden, celebrate their first Christmas in Minnesota. (Frontier Life; Holidays)

678 Shaw, Janet. *Meet Kirsten, an American Girl*. Pleasant, 1986. Gr. 4-5. Kirsten and her family come to Minnesota from Sweden in 1850. The trip had its hardships but they arrive safe and sound. (Frontier Life; Family)

679 Turngren, Ellen. *Hearts Are the Fields*. McKay, 1961. Gr. 7- . Nils and Lovissa have problems as immigrant parents. They adjust to new ways but the generational conflict is difficult. (Generation Gap)

680 Wiberg, Harold. *Christmas at the Tomten's Farm*. Coward, 1968. Gr. 3-4. The farm's watchful Tomten lends a quiet helping hand during the two days of the Swedish Christmas celebration when the regular farm chores must be attended to in addition to holiday festivities. (Holidays)

681 Winter, Jeanette. *Klara's New World*. Knopf, 1992. Gr. 8- . Klara and her family are newly arrived in America from Sweden. They face many hardships but know they will have a better life. (Family)

TAIWANESE

682 Hughes, Dean. *Play Off*. Knopf, 1991. Gr. 3-5. Lean is Taiwanese but plays baseball well, in spite of his small stature. Teamwork toward a common goal wins games. (Sports/Baseball)

683 Scarboro, Elizabeth. *Secret Language of the SB*. Viking, 1990. Gr. 4-6. Adam's home life is disrupted when Susan, a foster child, comes to stay while awaiting adoption. Adam adjusts to her and feels she is trying to adjust to him. (Foster Care; Boys, Pre-teen)

THAI

684 Sleater, William. *Spirit House*. Dutton, 1991. Gr. 7-9. Bia, a Thai exchange student, arrives to live with Julie's family. He is handsome but very different . . . and he believes in spirits. (Family; Ghosts)

TRINIDADIAN

See also WEST INDIAN

685 Burden-Patman, Denise. *Carnival*. Simon & Schuster, 1993. Gr. K-3. Rosa will play the steel drum in the calypso band. She is new in Brooklyn and doubts the carnival will be as nice as it was in Trinidad. (Cultural Traits; Holidays)

TURKISH

686 Francis, Dorothy. *Laugh at the Evil Eye*. Messner, 1970. Gr.

6-9. Aya Ersu arrived at the Millers' as an exchange student. Lisa was delighted until the conflict of cultures was so great that it affected both Aya and Lisa. But they both learn to understand. (Girls, Teen; Cultural Conflict)

UGANDAN

687 Kropp, Paul. *Fair Play.* EMC, 1982. Gr. 5-8. Carol accepts a party invitation from Andy, who is from Uganda. Her friends taunt her about it and make life uncomfortable for Andy. (Prejudice)

UKRAINIAN

688 Bloch, Marie. *Marya of Clark Avenue.* Coward, 1957. Gr. 5-8. Marya, nine, and her family keep the old traditions of Christmas and Easter. But at school she must adjust to the new ways. Finally the two ways of life blend and Marya is happy. (Girls, Pre-teen; Cultural Differences; Holidays)

689 Godden, Rumer. *Kitchen Madonna.* Viking, 1966. Gr. 5-8. Gregory and Janet were afraid they might lose their beloved maid, Marta, because she was unhappy. As Gregory builds a shrine for her, he changes from aloof and lonely to a new, happier person. (Family)

690 Polacco, Patricia. *Rechenka's Eggs.* Philomel, 1988. Gr. K-3. A story built around the wonderfully colored eggs the Ukrainians make at Christmas time. The story shows the intricate patterns of the Easter eggs. They reflect the colors of clothes, rugs, buildings, etc. (Holidays; Handicraft)

691 Polovchak, Walter. *Freedom's Choice.* Random, 1988. Gr. 7- . Natalie and Walter and their parents come to live in America. After six months the parents want to return to the Ukraine. Natalie and Walter run away because they don't want to go back. A controversial book. (Family; Generation Gap)

692 Skurzynski, Gloria. *Goodbye Billy Radish.* Bradbury, 1992. Gr. 4-7. Hank and Billy live in Pennsylvania during the First World War. Billy is Ukrainian and will work in the steel mills. Billy's death prompts Hank to get out of the steel mills and study to become a doctor. (Health & Medicine; Working World)

VIETNAMESE

693 Anderson, Rachel. *War Orphan.* Merrimack, 1986. Gr. 7- . Simon's family take in a Vietnamese war orphan named Ha. Simon learns a lot about the war and its effect on families by talking to Ha about his life in Vietnam.

694 Ashabranner, Brent. *Into a Strange Land.* Dodd, 1987. Gr. 6-9. A child is hidden in a boat heading for America. Upon arrival he is placed in a foster home where he must adjust to the loss of family and country. (Orphans; Foster Care)

Vietnamese (695)

695 Breckler, Rosemary. *Hoang Breaks the Lucky Teapot.* Houghton, 1992. Gr. K-3. Hoang tries to restore good luck to his household after he breaks the family's lucky teapot. Good Fortune leaves and Bad Fortune is in the home. He must get rid of the evil spirits and return Good Fortune. (Cultural Traits; Superstitions)

696 Brown, Tricia. *Lee Ann.* Putnam, 1991. Gr. 3-5. Lee Ann goes to elementary school, celebrates Tet, the Vietnamese New Year, is at home with family and friends and moves about in the community. (Girls, Pre-teen; Community Life)

697 Cebulash, Mel. *Carly and Co.* Ballantine, 1989. Gr. 7-9. Sandy, a Vietnamese boy, and Carly play detective in this lightweight mystery. (Mystery)

698 Coutant, Helen. *First Snow.* Knopf, 1974. Gr. K-3. Lein knows her grandmother is dying but does not know the meaning of death. Her grandmother tells her it is like the snowflakes, that even though one changes in one form one lives on in another. (Grandparents; Death)

699 Dixon, Paige. *Promises to Keep.* Atheneum, 1974. Gr. 7-9. Charles, 16, lives in a small town. Lin, a cousin, is part Vietnamese and comes to live in town. There is a great deal of prejudice. (Prejudice; Boys, Teen)

700 Dolgin, P. *Yin's Special Thanksgiving.* January Productions, 1985. Gr. K-2. Yin shares one of her favorite Vietnamese foods with her friends on her first Thanksgiving in America. (Food; Friendship)

701 Dunn, Marylois. *Absolutely Perfect Horse.* Harper, 1983. Gr. 7-9. Annie buys an old horse to keep it from being destroyed. The family baby is attacked by feral dogs and Annie and her horse rescue it. The horse later must be killed (by adopted Taro Chan), but Annie has good memories. (Horses, Trained; Courage)

702 Gilson, Jamie. *Hello, My Name Is Scrambled Eggs.* Lothrop, 1984. Gr. 4-6. Harvey, the school's best known student (for a number of different reasons), meets Tuan from Vietnam. His job? Make an American out of him! (Boys, Pre-teen; School)

703 Hoyt-Goldsmith, Diane. *Hoang Anh: Vietnamese-American.* Holiday House, 1991. Gr. 2-5. Hoang Anh arrived in America as a baby after his family escaped from Vietnam in a fishing boat. He learns to adjust to both cultures. (Boys, Pre-teen; Cultural Differences)

704 MacMillan, Dianne. *My Best Friend, Duc Tran.* Messner, 1987. Gr. 4-6. Eddie meets a young Vietnamese boy and they become friends. Eddie learns more about a country he knew little about. (Friendship Among Boys; Family)

705 Martin, Ann. *Yours Truly, Shirley.* Holiday House, 1988. Gr. 4-6. Shirley is dyslexic and feels inferior to her bright brother and adopted Vietnamese sister. (Handicapped; Siblings)

706 Moore, Ruth. *Mystery of the Missing Stallions.* Herald, 1984. Gr. 4-6. Sara and Sam find a Vietnamese refugee in an abandoned cabin. They also investigate the disappearance of thoroughbred horses from a nearby farm. (Brothers & Sisters; Mystery)

707 Paterson, Katherine. *Park's Quest.* Lodestar, 1988. Gr. 4-6. Park goes to his grandfather's farm. His father died in Vietnam and he wants to know more about him. While there he meets a Vietnamese-American. All he finds out about his father is unpleasant. (Fathers & Sons; Self-Esteem)

708 Reiff, Tana. *Boat People.* Fearon, 1989. Gr. 4-6. The Nguyen family left Vietnam in their small craft and went to Malaysia, Indonesia, and then to Texas, where they joined other fishermen from Vietnam. Life was not easy and there was conflict. (Cultural Conflict; Fish & Fishing)

709 Reiff, Tana. *Family from Vietnam.* Fearon, 1979. Gr. 4-7. Mai and Set and their three children are separated as they try to get a plane for the United States. Set and one son are left behind. They later are reunited but the one son dies. (Family)

710 Surat, Michele. *Angel Child, Dragon Child.* Raintree, 1983. Gr. K-2. Ut attends school in America. She misses her mother but makes a new good friend when he really listens to her story and relates it to the class. Then everyone better understands Ut's loneliness. (School; Lonesomeness)

711 Tran, Kim-Lan. *Tet: The New Year.* Simon & Schuster, 1993. Gr. 3-5. Huy-Ly and his father miss Vietnam and do not want to participate in the New Year's celebrations away from home. But Huy-Ly's teacher convinces them they should. Basic information about this holiday. (Holidays; Fathers & Sons)

712 Tran-Khanh-Tuyet. *Little Weaver of Thai-Yen Village.* Children's, 1987. Gr. K-3. Hien is wounded and orphaned during the Vietnamese war and is brought to America for both hospital care and a new life. She weaves blankets with the spirit bird on each and sends them to the needy. (Orphans; Loyalty; Handicrafts)

713 Turner, Ann Warren. *Through Moon and Stars and Night Skies.* Harper, 1990. Gr. K-2. An orphaned boy is being adopted and is flying to his new home and parents he has never seen. He is both excited and scared. (Adoption)

714 Wartski, Maureen. *Long Way from Home.* Westminster, 1980. Gr. 5-8. Kien comes to America from Vietnam. He does not adjust well. He moves to another town but still faces prejudice. He becomes a hero by saving the town's leader from a fire. (Prejudice; Courage)

WEST INDIAN

See also BAHAMIAN, BARBADIAN, CUBAN, DOMINICAN, PUERTO RICAN, TRINIDADIAN

715 Guy, Rosa. *Friends.* Bantam, 1973. Gr. 7-9. Phyllisa leaves the West Indies to live in New York. She has a difficult time until she meets Edith, a street child, and together they make their way. (Siblings; Friendship Among Girls)

716 White, Edgar. *Sati, the Rastafarian.* Lothrop, 1973. Gr. K-2. Sati misses the sounds and sights of his homeland, but he makes friends with the children of dancers and musicians and is less homesick. (Urban Life; Lonesomeness)

YUGOSLAVIAN

717 Shapiro, Irwin. *Joe Magarac and His U.S.A. Citizenship Papers.* Univ. of Pittsburgh Press, 1979. Gr. 5-8. A tall tale told with humor about the plight of "greenhorns" and the contribution immigrants made to the wealth of the United States. (Humorous, Citizenship)

Appendix: Books Arranged by Grade Level

Grades K-2

Asian

Javernick, Ellen	*Where's Brooke*
McDaniel, Becky B.	*Katie Can*
McDaniel, Becky B.	*Katie Couldn't*
McDaniel, Becky B.	*Katie Did It*

Chinese

Ashley, Bernard	*Cleversticks*
Behrens, June	*Soo Ling Finds a Way*
Buck, Pearl	*Chinese Story Teller*
Bunting, Eve	*Happy Funeral*
McCunn, Ruthanne	*Pie-biter*
Molnar, Joe	*Sherman*
Politi, Leo	*Mr. Fong's Toy Shop*
Stock, Catherine	*Emma's Dragon Hunt*

Czechoslovakian

Addy, Sharon	*Visit with Great-Grandma*

Dutch

Monjo, F.N.	*Rudi and the Distelfink*

Finnish

Worchester, Gurdon	*Singing Flute*

Hispanic

Fern, Eugene	*Pepito's Story*
Weiss, Nicki	*On a Hot, Hot Day*

Italian

Dionetti, Michelle — *Coal Mine Peaches*

Japanese

Battles, Edith — *What Does the Rooster Say, Yoshio?*
Bonner, Louise — *What's My Name in Hawaii?*
Garrison, Christian — *Dream Eater*
Hawkinson, Lucy — *Dance, Dance, Amy-Chan*
Taylor, Mark — *Time for Flowers*
Yashima, Mitsu — *Momo's Kitten*

Korean

Johnson, Doris — *SuAn*
Sobol, Harriet — *We Don't Look Like Our Mom and Dad*

Mexican

Adams, Ruth J. — *Fidelia*
Babbitt, Lorraine — *Pink Like the Geranium*
Behrens, June — *Fiesta!*
Embry, Margaret — *Peg-Leg Willy*
Frazier, James — *Los Posadas*
Freeman, Don — *Friday Surprise*
Hitte, Kathryn — *Mexicali Soup*
Jaynes, Ruth — *Melinda's Christmas Stocking*
Jaynes, Ruth — *Tell Me Please, What's That*
Jaynes, Ruth — *What Is a Birthday Child*
Marzollo, Jean — *Soccer Sam*
Mora, Pat — *Birthday Basket for Tia*
Ormsby, Virginia — *Twenty-One Children Plus Ten*
Ormsby, Virginia — *What's Wrong with Julio?*
Politi, Leo — *Pedro, Angel of Olvera Street*
Prieto, Marlana — *When the Monkeys Wore Sombreros*
Williams, Vera — *Chair for My Mother*
Williams, Vera — *Music, Music for Everyone*
Williams, Vera — *Something Special for Me*

Puerto Rican

Blue, Rose	*I Am Here: You Estoy Agui*
Greene, Roberta	*Two and Me Makes Three*
Keats, Ezra	*My Dog Is Lost!*
Lexau, Joan	*Maria*
Molnar, Joe	*Elizabeth*
Solbert, Ronnie	*I Wrote My Name on the Wall*
Sonneborn, Ruth	*Friday Night Is Papa Night*
Sonneborn, Ruth	*Lollipop Party*
Sonneborn, Ruth	*Seven in Bed*

Russian

Caseley, Judith	*Apple Pie and Onions*
Chec, John	*My Grandmother's Journey*
Heller, Linda	*Castle on Hester Street*
Polacco, Patricia	*Keeping Quilt*

Vietnamese

Dolgin, P.	*Yin's Special Thanksgiving*
Surat, Michele	*Angel Child, Dragon Child*
Turner, Ann Warren	*Through Moon and Stars and Night Skies*

West Indian

White, Edgar	*Sati, the Rastafarian*

Grades K-3

Albanian

Tashjian, Virginia	*Once There Was and Was Not*

Chinese

Cheng, Hou-Tien *Chinese New Year*
Lee, Helen *My Grandfather and Me*
Waters, Kate *Lion Dancer: Ernie Wan's Chinese New Year*
Yee, Paul *Roses Sing on New Show*

Dutch

Howe, John *Rip Van Winkle*
Milhous, Katherine *Egg Tree*

English

Hoguet, Susan *Solomon Grundy*

German

Levoy, Myron *Hanukkah of Great-Uncle Otto*
Rowland, Florence *Amish Wedding*

Greek

Brandenberg, Aliki *Eggs: Green Folk Tale*

Italian

Miles, Betty *Feast on Sullivan Street*

Japanese

Friedman, Ina *How My Parents Learned to Eat*
Uchida, Yoshiko *Birthday Visitor*

Korean

Kline, Suzy *Horrible Harry's Secret*
Macmillan, Dianne *My Best Friend, Mee-Yung*
Pellegrini, Nina *Families Are Different*
Rosenberg, Maxine *My Friend Leslie*

Mexican

Anaya, Rudolfo	*Farolitos of Christmas*
Atkinson, Mary	*Maria Teresa*
Bolognese, Don	*New Day*
Brown, Tricia	*Hello, Amigos!*
Cruz, Manuel	*Chicano Christmas Story*
Havill, Juanita	*Treasure Nap*
Hewett, Joan	*Laura Loves Horses*
Maury, Inez	*My Mother and I Are Growing Strong*
Maury, Inez	*My Mother the Mail Carrier*
Politi, Leo	*Nicest Gift*
Politi, Leo	*Three Stalks of Corn*
Roe, Eileen	*With My Brother (Con mi Hermano)*
Schoberle, Cecile	*Esmeralda and the Pet Parade*
Taha, Karen	*Gift for Tia Rosa*
Texter, Sylvia	*We Laughed a Lot, My First Day of School*

Polish

Leighton, Maxinne	*Ellis Island Christmas*
Lenski, Lois	*We Live in the North*
Waterton, Betty	*Petranella*

Puerto Rican

Binzen, William	*Carmen*
Binzen, William	*Miguel's Mountain*
Bourne, M.	*Emilio's Summer Day*
Hearn, Emily	*Around Another Corner*
Kesselman, Wendy	*Angelita*
Kuklin, Susan	*How My Family Lives in America*
McCabe, Inger	*Week in Henry's World*
Martel, Cruz	*Yagua Days*
Reit, Seymour	*Dear Uncle Carlos*
Talbot, Toby	*My House Is Your House*
Thomas, Dawn	*Mira! Mira!*

Russian

Gelfand, Marilyn	*My Great-Grandpa Joe*
Polacco, Patricia	*Thunder Cake*
Polacco, Patricia	*Uncle Vova's Tree*

Scottish

De Mejo, Oscar	*Forty-Niners*

Senegalese

Kuklin, Susan	*How My Family Lives in America*

Trinidadian

Burden-Patman, Denise	*Carnival*

Ukrainian

Polacco, Patricia	*Rechenka's Eggs*

Vietnamese

Breckler, Rosemary	*Hoang Breaks the Lucky Teapot*
Coutant, Helen	*First Snow*
Tran-Khanh-Tuyet	*Little Weaver of Thai-Yen Village*

Grades 1-3

Chinese

Pinkwater, Daniel	*Wingman*
Politi, Leo	*Moy Moy*

Dutch

Moskin, Marietta	*Lysbet and the Fire Kitten*

Japanese

Bang, Molly	*Paper Crane*
Copeland, Helen	*Meet Miki Takino*

Mexican

Gray, Genevieve — *How Far, Felipe?*
Politi, Leo — *Juanita*

Puerto Rican

Thomas, Dawn — *Pablito's New Feet*

Russian

Cohen, Barbara — *Gooseberries to Oranges*

Swedish

Sandin, Joan — *Long Way to a New Land*
Sandin, Joan — *Long Way Westward*

Grades 1-4

Chinese

Keating, Norma — *Mr. Chu*

Japanese

Politi, Leo — *Mieko*

Mexican

Williams, Vera — *Stringbean's Trip to the Shining Sea*

Puerto Rican

Belpre, Pura — *Santiago*

Grades 2-4

Albanian

Cretan, Gladys — *All Except Sammy*

Chinese

Anderson, Juanita	*Charley Yee's New Year*
Chang, Heidi	*Elaine and the Flying Frog*
Coerr, Eleanor	*Chang's Paper Pony*
Levine, Ellen	*I Hate English!*

Cuban

Prieto, Mariana	*Johnny Lost*

Czechoslovakian

Mitchell, Barbara	*Tomahawks and Trombones*

Ecuadoran

Wainwright, Richard	*Mountains to Climb*

French

Hays, Wilma	*Open Gate: New Year's 1815*

Korean

Paek, Min	*Aekyung's Dream*

Lebanese

Shefelman, Janice	*Peddler's Dream*

Mexican

Ets, Marie	*Bad Boy, Good Boy*
Politi, Leo	*Mission Bell*
Politi, Leo	*Song of the Swallows*

Puerto Rican

Barth, Edna	*Day Luis Was Lost*

Russian

Clark, Margery — *Poppy Seed Cakes*
Harvey, Brett — *Immigrant Girl*

Grades 2-5

Chinese

Martin, Patricia — *Rice Bowl Pet*

Mexican

Bruni, Mary Ann — *Rosita's Christmas Wish*
Hewett, Joan — *Hector Lives in the United States*

Russian

Cohen, Barbara — *Molly's Pilgrim*

Vietnamese

Hoyt-Goldsmith, Diane — *Hoang Anh: Vietnamese-American*

Grades 3-4

Chilean

Molarsky, Osmond — *Different Ball Game*

Chinese

Evans, Doris — *Mr. Charley's Chopsticks*
Lim, Genny — *Wings for Lai Ho*

Dutch

Mitchell, Barbara — *Old Fasnacht*

German

Lehmann, Linda — *Better Than a Princess*

Greek

Aiello, Barbara — *Portrait of Me*

Hispanic

Anderson, Eloise — *Carlos Goes to School*

Japanese

Uchida, Yoshiko — *Rooster That Understood Japanese*

Korean

Beirne, Barbara — *Pianist's Debut*

Polish

Sendak, Philip — *In Grandpa's House*

Puerto Rican

Burchard, Peter — *Chito*
Shearer, J. — *Little Man in the Family*

Swedish

Shaw, Janet — *Happy Birthday, Kirsten!*
Wiberg, Harold — *Christmas at the Tomten's Farm*

Grades 3-5

Bahamian

Prieto, Mariana — *Tomato Boy*

Chinese

Bales, Carol Ann — *Chinatown Sunday*
Buck, Pearl — *Chinese Children Next Door*
Chang, Heidi — *Elaine, Mary Lewis, and the Frogs*

Cuban

Holland, Isabelle — *Amanda's Choice*

Danish

Kerr, Helen — *Helga's Magic*

Dutch

St. George, Judith — *Shad Are Running*

Irish

Sawyer, Ruth — *Roller Skates*

Italian

Sawyer, Ruth — *Roller Skates*

Mexican

Galbraith, Clare — *Victor*
Gee, Maurice — *Chicano, Amigo*
Smith, Mary Lou — *Grandmother's Adobe Dollhouse*
Stanek, Muriel — *I Speak English for My Mom*

Puerto Rican

Brenner, Barbara — *Barto Takes the Subway*
Burchardt, Nellie — *Surprise for Carlotta*
Figueroa, John — *Antonio's World*
Lexau, Joan — *Jose's Christmas Secret*
Prieto, Mariana — *Tomato Boy*
Talbot, Charlene — *Tomas Takes Charge*

Russian

Tolstoy, Leo — *Lion and the Puppy*

Taiwanese

Hughes, Dean — *Play Off*

Vietnamese

Brown, Tricia *Lee Ann*
Tran, Kim-Lan *Tet: The New Year*

Grades 3 – 6

English

Bulla, Clyde *Lion to Guard Us*
Chessman, Ruth *Bound for Freedom*

French

Crayder, Teresa *Cathy and Lisette*

German

Leviton, Sonia *Silver Days*

Japanese

Hayes, Florence *Boy in the 49th Seat*

Korean

Sinykin, Sheri *Buddy Trap*

Mexican

Hood, Flora *One Luminaria for Antonia*

Puerto Rican

Lewiton, Mina *Candita's Choice*
Mann, Peggy *When Carlos Closed the Street*

Grades 4 – 5

Chinese

Reit, Seymour *Rice Cakes and Paper Dragons*

Dutch

Edmonds, Walter — *Matchlock Gun*

English

Bulla, Clyde — *Charlie's House*

German

De Angeli, Marguerite — *Skippack School*

Italian

Bylinksy, Tatyana — *Before the Wild Flowers Bloom*

Japanese

Yashima, Taro — *Youngest One*

Mexican

Wolf, Bernard — *In This Proud Land*

Portuguese

Foltz, Mary Jane — *Nicolau's Prize*

Puerto Rican

Bouchard, Lois — *Boy Who Wouldn't Talk*
Mann, Peggy — *Clubhouse*

Russian

Maguire, Gregory — *Daughter of the Moon*

Scottish

Hays, Wilma — *Highland Halloween*

Swedish

Shaw, Janet — *Changes for Kirsten*
Shaw, Janet — *Kirsten Learns a Lesson*

Grades 4-6

Albanian

Cretan, Gladys	*Sunday for Sona*
Kherdian, David	*Song for Uncle Harry*

Australian

Wrightson, Patricia	*Little Fear*

Chinese

Estes, Eleanor	*Lost Umbrella of Kim Chu*
Howard, Ellen	*Her Own Song*
Lenski, Lois	*San Francisco Boy*
Lord, Bette	*In the Year of the Boar and Jackie Robinson*
Namioka, Lensey	*Yang the Youngest and His Terrible Ear*
Newman, Shirlee P.	*Yellow Silk for May Lee*
Say, Allen	*El Chino*
Wyndham, Robert	*Tales the People Tell in China*
Yep, Laurence	*Child of the Owl*
Yep, Laurence	*Sea Glass*
Yep, Laurence	*Star Fisher*

Cuban

Bishop, Curtis	*Little League Amigo*
Pesera, Hilda	*Cuban Boy's Adventures in America*

Czechoslovakian

Moore, Ruth	*Peace Treaty*

Shaw, Janet — *Kirsten Saves the Day*
Shaw, Janet — *Kirsten's Surprise*
Shaw, Janet — *Meet Kirsten, an American Girl*

Danish

Olsen, Violet — *View from the Pighouse Roof*

Dutch

Irving, Washington — *Rip Van Winkle and the Legend of Sleepy Hollow*
Spicer, Dorothy — *Owl's Nest*

English

Finlayson, Ann — *Greenhorn of the Frontier*
Jensen, Pauline — *Thicker Than Water*

European

Rosenberg, Liz — *Grandmother and the Runaway Shadow*

Finnish

Clark, Ann Nolan — *All This Wild Land*

French

Clark, Ann Nolan — *Paco's Miracle*

German

Baker, Betty — *Dunderhead War*
Colver, Anne — *Bread and Butter Indian*
Fleming, Alice — *King of Prussia and a Peanut Butter Sandwich*
Fletcher, Susan — *Stuttgart Nanny Mafia*
Hickman, Janet — *Stones*
Hoff, Carol — *Johnny Texas*
Hurwitz, Johanna — *Once I Was a Plum Tree*
Jordan, Mildred — *Proud to Be Amish*
Keehn, Sally — *I Am Regina*
Lehmann, Linda — *Tilli's New World*
Selz, Irma — *Katy, Be Good*
Shefelman, Janice — *Paradise Called Texas*
Shefelman, Janice — *Spirit of Iron*
Walley, Constance — *Six Generations*
Weiman, Eiveen — *Which Way Courage?*
Williamson, Joanne — *And Forever Free*

Greek

George, Harry — *Demo of 70th Street*
Lord, Athena — *Luck of Z.A.P. and Zoe*
Lord, Athena — *Today's Special Z.A.P. and Zoe*

Hispanic

Carlstrom, Nancy — *Light: Story of a Small Kindness*
Holman, Felice — *Secret City, U.S.A.*

Irish

Allan, Mabel — *Bridge of Friendship*
Curley, Daniel — *Billy Beg and the Bull*
Fisher, Leonard — *Across the Sea from Galway*
Giff, Patricia — *Gift of the Pirate Queen*
Shura, Mary — *Shoe Full of Shamrock*
Stolz, Mary — *Noonday Friends*
Talbot, Charlene — *Orphan for Nebraska*

Italian

Gross, Virginia — *It's Only Goodbye*
Panetta, George — *Shoeshine Boys*
Paul, Louis — *Papa Luigi's Marionettes*

Japanese

Bonham, Frank — *Mystery in Little Tokyo*
Cavanna, Betty — *Jenny Kimura*
Christopher, Matt — *Shortstop from Tokyo*
Cox, William — *Trouble at Second Base*
Haugaard, Kay — *Myeko's Gift*
Inyart, Gene — *Jenny*
Uchida, Yoshiko — *Best Bad Things*
Uchida, Yoshiko — *Happiest Ending*
Uchida, Yoshiko — *Jar of Dreams*
Uchida, Yoshiko — *Journey Home*
Uchida, Yoshiko — *Journey to Topaz*
Uchida, Yoshiko — *Mik and the Prowler*
Uchida, Yoshiko — *Promised Year*

Korean

Choc, Book Nyul — *Halmoni*
McDonald, Joyce — *Mail-Order Kid*

Melanesian

Goodwin, Harold — *Cargo*

Mexican

Anderson, Joan — *Spanish Pioneers of the Southwest*
Beatty, Patricia — *Lupita Manana*
Beckett, Hilary — *My Brother, Angel*
Bishop, Curtis — *Little League Double Play*
Blue, Rose — *We Are Chicano*
Brenner, Barbara — *Mystery of the Disappearing Dogs*
Bulla, Clyde — *Benito*
Clark, Ann Nolan — *Paco's Miracle*
Cox, William — *Trouble at Second Base*
De Leon, Nephtali — *I Will Catch the Sun*
Dunne, Mary — *Reach Out, Ricardo*
Fall, Thomas — *Wild Boy*
Fink, Augusta — *To Touch the Sky*
Fulle, Suzanne — *Lanterns for Fiesta*
Garthwaite, Marion — *Mario*
Gault, William — *Trouble at Second*
Gerson, Corinne — *Oh, Brother!*
Gray, Patsey — *Flag Is Up*
Greene, Constance — *Manuel, Young Mexican American*
Laklan, Carli — *Migrant Girl*
MacMillan, Dianne — *My Best Friend, Martha Rodriguez*
Martin, Patricia — *Grandma's Gun*
Molnar, Joe — *Graciela*
Paul, Paula — *You Can Hear a Magpie Smile*
Roldan, Fernando — *Kite*
Roy, Cal — *Serpent and the Sun*
Schaefer, Jack — *Old Ramon*
Soto, Gary — *Skirt*
Soto, Gary — *Taking Sides*
Taylor, Theodore — *Maldonado Miracle*

Norwegian

Archer, Marion — *There Is a Happy Land*

Pakistani

Andrews, Jean — *Secret in the Dorm Attic*
Parker, Richard — *Boy Who Wasn't Lonely*

Peruvian

Molloy, Anne — *Girl from Two Miles High*

Polish

Estes, Eleanor — *Hundred Dresses*
Holman, Felice — *Murderer*
Kushner, Donn — *Uncle Jacob's Ghost Story*
Pellowski, Anne — *Betsy's Up-and-Down Year*
Pellowski, Anne — *Willow Wind Farm: Betsy's Story*

Portuguese

Newman, Shirlee P. — *Shipwrecked Dog*
Patton, Willoughby — *Manuel's Discovery*

Puerto Rican

Bonham, Frank — *Mystery of the Fat Cat*
Campion, Wardi — *Casa Means Home*
Christopher, Matt — *Baseball Flyhawk*
Garcia, Richard — *My Aunt Otilia's Spirits*
Gray, Genevieve — *Dark Side of Nowhere*
Heuman, William — *Little League Hotshots*
Hurwitz, Johanna — *Class President*
Lewiton, Mina — *That Bad Carlos*
Mann, Peggy — *How Juan Got Home*
Mann, Peggy — *Street of the Flower Boxes*
Mohr, Nicholasa — *Felita*
Moore, Ruth — *Tomas and the Talking Birds*

Shotwell, Louisa — *Magdalena*
Shyer, Marlene — *Tino*
Speevack, Yetta — *Spider Plant*
Thaler, Susan — *Rosaria*
Weiner, Sandra — *They Call Me Jack*

Russian

Christopher, Matt — *Look Who's Playing First Base*
Crayder, Dorothy — *Joker and the Swan*
Curley, Daniel — *Hilarion*
Forman, Marcey — *Russian in the Attic*
Lehrman, Robert — *Store That Mama Built*
McLerran, Alice — *Secrets*
Moskin, Marietta — *Waiting for Mama*
Nathan, Dorothy — *Shy One*

Scottish

Buchan, Bryan — *Copper Sunrise*

Swedish

Christgau, Alice — *Runaway to Glory*
Lindquist, Jennie — *Golden Name Day*
Lindquist, Jennie — *Little Silver House*
Norris, Gunella — *Feast of Light*

Taiwanese

Scarboro, Elizabeth — *Secret Language of the SB*

Vietnamese

Gilson, Jamie — *Hello, My Name Is Scrambled Eggs*
MacMillan, Dianne — *My Best Friend, Duc Tran*
Martin, Ann — *Yours Truly, Shirley*
Moore, Ruth — *Mystery of the Missing Stallions*
Paterson, Katherine — *Park's Quest*
Reiff, Tana — *Boat People*

Grades 4-7

Australian

Wier, Ester — *Rumptydoolers*

Chinese

Chetin, Helen — *Angel Island Prisoner*
La Rouche, Adelle — *Binkey and the Bamboo Brush*
Reiff, Tana — *For Gold and Blood*

Cuban

Reiff, Tana — *Different Home*

English

Crompton, Anne — *Ice Trail*

European

Reiff, Tana — *Old Way, New Ways*

French

Reiff, Tana — *Chicken by Che*

German

Reiff, Tana — *O Little Town*

Irish

Reiff, Tana — *Hungry No More*

Italian

Reiff, Tana — *Door Is Open*
Reiff, Tana — *Little Italy*

Japanese

Savin, Marcia — *Moon Bridge*

Mexican

Lomas Garza, Carmen — *Family Pictures*
Place, Marian — *Juan's 18 Wheeler Summer*
Reiff, Tana — *Magic Paper*

Norwegian

Reiff, Tana — *Push to the West*

Puerto Rican

Gonzalez, Gloria — *Gaucho*
Sachs, Marilyn — *Truth About Mary Rose*

Ukrainian

Skurzynski, Gloria — *Good-bye Billy Radish*

Vietnamese

Reiff, Tana — *Family from Vietnam*

Grades 5-8

African

Sterne, Emma — *Long Black Schooner*

Albanian

Drizari, Nelo — *Four Seas to Dreamland*

Australian

Phipson, Joan — *When the City Stopped*

Burmese

Law-Yone, Wendy — *Coffin Tree*

Chinese

Namioka, Lensey — *Who's Hu?*
Robertson, Keith — *Year of the Jeep*

Terris, Susan — *Latchkey Kids*
Yep, Laurence — *Serpent's Children*

Cuban

Cox, William — *Game, Set and Match*

Czechoslovakian

Barker, Mary — *Milenka's Happy Summer*
Drdek, Richard — *Game*
Moore, Ruth — *Christmas Surprise*
Moore, Ruth — *Distant Thunder*

English

Constiner, Merle — *Sumatra Alley*
Hall, Marjory — *Other Girl*
Harris, Christie — *West with the White Chiefs*
Ish-Kishor, Sul — *Our Eddie*
Wisler, G. Clifton — *This New Land*

European

Krumgold, Joseph — *Onion John*

Finnish

Adair, Margaret — *Far Voice Calling*

French

Jackson, Jacqueline — *Taste of Spruce Gum*

German

Gurasich, Marj — *Letters to Oma*
Withey, Barbara — *Serpent Ring*

Greek

Foley, June — *Falling in Love Is No Snap*

Hungarian

Line, David — *Soldier and Me*

Irish

Bolton, Carole — *Search of Mary Katherine Mulloy*
Branson, Karen — *Streets of Gold*
Conlon-McKenna, Marita — *Wildflower Girl*
Cummings, Betty — *Now, Ameriky*
Fenton, Edward — *Duffy's Rock*
Yates, Elizabeth — *Hue and Cry*

Italian

Angelo, Valenti — *Golden Gate*
Jackson, Jacqueline — *Taste of Spruce Gum*

Japanese

Uchida, Yoshiko — *Samurai of Gold Hill*

Korean

Lee, Marie — *Finding My Voice*
Lee, Marie — *If It Hadn't Been for Yoon Jun*

Latvian

Balch, Glenn — *Runaways*

Mexican

Beckett, Hilary — *Rafael and the Raiders*
Bethancourt, T.E. — *Me Inside of Me*
Bograd, Larry — *Fourth Grade Dinosaur Club*
Bonham, Frank — *Viva Chicano*
Cardenas, Leo — *Return to Ramos*
Colman, Hila — *Chicago Girl*
Dunnahoo, Terry — *This Is Espie Sanchez*
Dunnahoo, Terry — *Who Cares About Espie Sanchez?*
Dunnahoo, Terry — *Who Needs Espie Sanchez?*

Gates, Doris	*Blue Willow*
Hamilton, Dorothy	*Anita's Choice*
Krumgold, Joseph	*...And Now Miguel*
Marvin, Isabel	*Josefina and the Hanging Tree*
Reed, Fran	*Dream with Storms*
Strange, Celia	*Foster Mary*
Warren, Mary	*Shadow of the Valley*
Young, Bob	*Good-bye, Amigos*

Norwegian

Dahl, Borghild	*Under This Roof*
Paulsen, Gary	*Winter Room*

Polish

Chase, Mary	*Journey to Boston*
Evernden, Margery	*Dream Keeper*
Hotze, Sollace	*Summer Endings*
Pellowski, Anne	*First Farm in the Valley: Anna's Story*
Pellowski, Anne	*Stairstep Farm: Anna Rose's Story*
Pellowski, Anne	*Winding Valley Farm: Annie's Story*

Puerto Rican

Crane, Caroline	*Don't Look at Me That Way*
Figueroa, Pablo	*Enrique*
Fleischman, H. Samuel	*Gang Girl*
Hall, Lynn	*Danza*
Heuman, William	*City High Champion*
Mohr, Nicholasa	*Going Home*
Shotwell, Louisa	*Adam Bookout*

Russian

Bernstein, Joanne	*Dmitry: A Young Soviet Immigrant*
Farrar, Susan C.	*Samantha on Stage*
Fine, Anne	*Granny Project*
Lelchuk, Alan	*On Home Ground*
Nixon, Joan	*Land of Hope*

Roseman, Kenneth *Melting Pot*
Sachs, Marilyn *Call Me Ruth*
Vineberg, Ethel *Grandmother Came from Dworitz*
Williams, Jeanne *Winter Wheat*

Scottish

Capron, Louis *Red War Pole*
Weller, Frances *Boat Song*

Senegalese

O'Dell, Scott *My Name Is Not Angelica*

Spanish

Clark, Ann Nolan *Year Walk*

Swedish

Johnson, Lois W. *Trouble at Wild River*

Ugandan

Kropp, Paul *Fair Play*

Ukrainian

Bloch, Marie *Marya of Clark Avenue*
Godden, Rumer *Kitchen Madonna*

Vietnamese

Wartski, Maureen *Long Way from Home*

Yugoslavian

Shapiro, Irwin *Joe Magarac and His U.S.A. Citizenship Papers*

Grades 6-9

Chinese

Haugaard, Kay — *China Boy*
Yep, Laurence — *Rainbow People*

French

Kerle, Arthur — *Whispering Trees*
Klein, Norma — *Bizou*
Levoy, Myron — *Alan and Naomi*

German

Murray, Michelle — *Crystal Nights*

Hungarian

Christopher, Matt — *21 Mile Swim*

Mexican

O'Dell, Scott — *Child of Fire*
Summers, James — *Don't Come Back a Stranger*
Whitney, Phyllis — *Long Time Coming*

Norwegian

Dahl, Borghild — *Good News*

Turkish

Francis, Dorothy — *Laugh at the Evil Eye*

Vietnamese

Ashabranner, Brent — *Into a Strange Land*

Grades 7-

Barbadian

Marshall, Paule — *Brown Girl, Brownstones*

Czechoslovakian

Cather, Willa — *My Ántonia*
Skurzynski, Gloria — *Tempering*

El Salvadoran

Buss, Fran — *Journey of the Sparrows*

English

Williamson, Joanne — *Glorious Conspiracy*

French

Peck, Robert — *Fawn*
Pundt, Helen — *Spring Comes First to the Willows*

German

Fährmann, Willi — *Long Journey of Lucas B.*

Greek

O'Dell, Scott — *Alexandra*

Hungarian

Anderson, Mary — *That's Not My Style*
Konigsburg, E.L. — *Throwing Shadows*
Lewiton, Mina — *Elizabeth and the Young Stranger*

Indian

Mukherjee, Bharati — *Tiger's Daughter*

Italian

Granger, Peg — *After the Picnic*
Mangione, Jerre — *Mount Allegro*

Japanese

Breckenfeld, Vivian — *Two Worlds of Noriko*
Kanazawa, Tooru — *Sushi and Sourdough*
Sugimoto, E.I. — *Daughter of the Samurai*

Mexican

Diaz, Paul	*Up from El Paso*
Griego, Jose & Maestas	*Cuentos: Tales from the Hispanic Southwest*
Heuman, William	*City High Five*
Ogan, Margaret	*Tennis Bum*
Schellie, Don	*Maybe Next Summer*
Summers, James	*You Can't Make It by Bus*
Trivelpiece, Laurel	*During Water Peaches*

Norwegian

Anderson, Mary	*Who Says Nobody's Perfect?*
Cather, Willa	*O Pioneers!*
Rolvaag, Ole	*Boat of Longing*

Polish

Asch, Sholem	*Mother*
Janney, Russell	*Miracle of the Bells*
Mark, Michael	*Toba at the Hands of a Thief*

Puerto Rican

Colman, Hila	*Girl from Puerto Rico*
Melendez, Carmello	*Long Time Growing*

Russian

Angell, Judie	*One-Way to Ansonia*
Geras, Adele	*Voyage*
Lasky, Kathryn	*Night Journey*
Papashvily, George	*Home and Home Again*

Spanish

McGiffin, Lee	*Riders of Enchanted Valley*
Price, Eugenia	*Don Juan McQueen*

Swedish

Moberg, Vilhelm — *Emigrants*
Turngren, Ellen — *Hearts Are the Fields*

Ukrainian

Polovchak, Walter — *Freedom's Child*

Vietnamese

Anderson, Rachel — *War Orphan*

Grades 7-9

Albanian

Kherdian, David — *Asking the River*
Kherdian, David — *Road from Home: Story of an Armenian Girl*

Belgian

Rose, Anne — *Refugee*

Cambodian

Betancourt, Jeanne — *More Than Meets the Eye*
Crew, Linda — *Children of the River*

Chinese

Benezra, Barbara — *Fire Dragon*
Gregory, Diana — *One Boy at a Time*
Kingston, Maxine H. — *Woman Warrior*
Lee, Gus — *China Boy*
Niemeyer, Marie — *Moon Guitar*
Pascal, Francine — *Out of Reach*
Ruby, Lois — *This Old Man*
Wong, Shawn — *Homebase*
Yep, Laurence — *Dragonwings*
Young, Ailda — *Land of the Iron Dragon*

Cuban

Mills, Claudia — *Luisa's American Dream*

Czechoslovakian

Hickman, Janet — *Valley of the Shadow*

Dutch

De Jong, Dola — *By Marvelous Agreement*
Gibbs, Alonzo — *Fields Breathe Sweet*

English

Avi — *True Confessions of Charlotte Doyle*
Beatty, Patricia — *Queen's Own Grove*
Clarke, Mary — *Iron Peacock*

Finnish

Miller, Helen — *Kirsti*

French

Erdman, Loula — *Room to Grow*
Field, Rachel — *Calico Bush*
Murphy, Barbara — *One Another*

German

Benary-Isbert, Margot — *Long Way Home*
Fast, Howard — *Immigrants*
Fife, Dale — *Walk a Narrow Bridge*
Hickman, Janet — *Zoar Blue*
Keith, Harold — *Obstinate Land*
Kerr, M.E. — *Him She Loves?*
Weaver, Robert — *Nice Guy, Go Home*
Weik, Mary — *House on Liberty Street*

Hispanic

Bradford, Richard — *Red Sky at Morning*

Hungarian

Hinchman, Catherine — *Torchlight*
Tamar, Erika — *It Happened at Cecilia's*

Irish

Branson, Karen	*Potato Eaters*
Harris, Christie	*Forbidden Frontier*
Irwin, Hadley	*Kim/Kimi*
Lawson, Robert	*Great Wheel*
Perez, Norah	*Passage*

Italian

Benasutti, Marion	*No Steady Job for Papa*
Bethancourt, T.E.	*New York City, Too Far from Tampa Blues*
Fisher, Leonard	*Letters from Italy*
Fletcher, David	*King's Goblet*
LeRoy, Gen	*Hotheads*
Marangell, Virginia	*Gianna Mia*
Mays, Lucinda	*Other Shore*

Japanese

Bonham, Frank	*Burma Rifles*
Irwin, Hadley	*Kim/Kimi*
Miklowitz, Gloria	*War Between the Classes*
Okimoto, Jean	*Molly by Any Other Name*

Korean

Betancourt, Jeanne	*More Than Meets the Eye*

Mexican

Bishop, Curtis	*Fast Break*
Cox, William	*Chicano Cruz*
Cox, William	*Third and Goal*
Hernandez, Irene	*Across the Great River*
Lampman, Evelyn	*Bandit of Mok Hill*
Lampman, Evelyn	*Go Up the Road*
Madison, Winifred	*Maria Luisa*
Means, Florence	*Us Maltbys*
Mills, Donia	*Long Way Home from Troy*
O'Dell, Scott	*Kathleen, Please Come Home*

Paulsen, Gary	*Sentries*
Ponce, Mary	*Wedding*
Rivera, Tomas	*And the Earth Did Not Devour Him*
Soto, Gary	*Baseball in April*
Steinbeck, John	*Tortilla Flat*
Van Der Veer, Judy	*Hold the Rein Free*
Villarreal, Jose	*Pocho*
Young, Bob	*Across the Tracks*

Norwegian

Dahl, Borghild	*Homecoming*

Puerto Rican

Bethancourt, T.E.	*New York City, Too Far from Tampa Blues*
Bethancourt, T.E.	*Where the Deer and the Cantaloupe Play*
Danska, Herbert	*Street Kids*
Gault, William	*Backfield Challenge*
Levoy, Myron	*Shadow Like a Leopard*
Means, Florence	*Us Maltbys*
Mohr, Nicholasa	*In Nueva York*
Mohr, Nicholasa	*Nilda*

Russian

Betancourt, Jeanne	*Home Sweet Home*
Blue, Rose	*Cold Rain on the Water*
Colman, Hila	*Rachel's Legacy*
Sherman, Eileen	*Independence Avenue*

Scottish

Clarke, Mary	*Iron Beacock*
Harris, Christie	*Forbidden Frontier*

Swedish

Ericson, Stig	*Dan Henry in the Wild West*

Thai

Sleater, William	*Spirit House*

Vietnamese

Cebulash, Mel	*Carly and Co.*
Dixon, Paige	*Promises to Keep*
Dunn, Marylois	*Absolutely Perfect Horse*

West Indian

Guy, Rosa	*Friends*

Grades 8 –

Chinese

Bennett, Jack	*Masks, a Love Story*
Li, Chin-Yang	*Land of the Golden Mountain*
Lo, Steven C.	*Incorporation of Eric Chung*
McCunn, Ruthanne	*Thousand Pieces of Gold*
Tan, Amy	*Joy Luck Club*
Tan, Amy	*Kitchen God's Wife*
Telemaque, Eleanor	*It's Crazy to Stay Chinese in Minnesota*
Wong, Jade Snow	*Fifth Chinese Daughter*

Dominican

Alvarez, Julia	*How the Garcia Girls Lost Their Accents*

Dutch

Plummer, Louise	*Romantic Obsessions and Humiliations*

English

Haugaard, Erik	*Orphans of the Wind*

German

Fast, Howard	*Immigrants Daughter*

Guatemalan

Kingsolver, Barbara	*Bean Trees*

Hispanic

Cisneros, Sandra	*House on Margo Street*

Irish

Nixon, Joan — *Land of Promise*

Italian

Christman, Elizabeth — *Nice Italian Girl*

Japanese

Houston, Jeanne — *Farewell to Manzanar*
Kadohata, Cynthia — *Floating World*
Okada, John — *No-No Boy*
Smith, Doris — *Salted Lemons*
Uchida, Yoshiko — *Picture Bride*
Yoshida, Jim — *Two Worlds of Jim Yoshida*

Mexican

Anaya, Rudolfo — *Bless Me, Ultima*
Anaya, Rudolfo — *Heart of Aztlan*
Cisneros, Sandra — *Woman Hollering Creek*
Dean, Karen — *Mariana*
Fernandez, Roberta — *Intaglio*
Galarza, Ernesto — *Barrio Boy*
Paredes, Americo — *George Washington Gomez*
Santiago, Danny — *Famous All Over Town*

Norwegian

Forbes, Kathryn — *Mama's Bank Account*

Russian

Cahan, Abraham — *Rise of David Levinsky*
Shiefman, Vicky — *Goodbye to the Trees*

Scottish

Watson, Sally — *Hornet's Nest*

Swedish

Budd, Lillian	*April Harvest*
Moberg, Vilhelm	*Unto a Good Land*
Winter, Jeanette	*Klara's New World*

Grades 9 -

Chinese

Chao, Evelina	*Gates of Grace*
Chin, Frank	*Donald Duk*
Lord, Bette	*Spring Moon*

Czechoslovakian

Kafka, Franz	*Amerika*

English

Breeding, Robert L.	*From London to Appalachia*
L'Engle, Madeline	*Other Side of the Sun*

Finnish

Cummings, Rebecca	*Kaisa Kliponen: Two Stories*

French

Hodge, Jane	*Savannah Purchase*

German

Asher, Carol	*Flood*
Fast, Howard	*Second Generation*
Good, Merle	*Happy as the Grass Was Green*
Mannix, Daniel	*Healer*
Tobenkin, Elias	*House of Conrad*

Greek

Janus, Christopher	*Miss Fourth of July, Goodbye*

Irish

Condon, Richard	*Mile High*
O'Connor, Edwin	*Edge of Sadness*
O'Connor, Edwin	*Last Hurrah*
Rowe, Jack	*Brandywine*

Italian

De Capite, Raymond	*Coming of Fabrizze*
De Capite, Raymond	*Lost King*
Di Donato, Pietro	*Christ in Concrete*
Di Donato, Pietro	*Three Circles in Light*
Forgione, Louis	*River Between*
Pagano, Jo	*Golden Wedding*
Parini, Jay	*Patch Boys*

Japanese

Charyn, Jerome	*American Scrapbook*
Irwin, Wallace	*Letters of a Japanese Schoolboy*

Lithuanian

Sinclair, Upton	*Jungle*

Mexican

Barrio, Edmond	*Plum Plum Pickers*
Chavez, Angelico	*Short Stories of Fray Angelico Chavez*
Cook, Bruce	*Mexican Standoff*
Garcia, Guy	*Skin Deep*
Hunter, Evan	*Walk Proud*
Vasquez, Richard	*Chicano*

Norwegian

Bojer, Johan	*Emigrants*
Rolvaag, Ole	*Their Father's God*
Rolvaag, Ole	*Third Life of Per Smevik*

Polish

Algren, Nelson	*Neon Wilderness*
Burt, Katherine	*Strong Citadel*
Fineman, Irving	*Hear, Ye Sons*

Fineman, Irving — *Hear, Ye Sons*
Roberts, Cecil — *One Small Candle*
Wisniowski, Sygurd — *Ameryka 100 Years Old*

Puerto Rican

Cofer, Judith — *Line of the Sun*
Cofer, Judith — *Silent Dancing*
Mohr, Nicholasa — *El Bronx Remembered*
Rivera, Edward — *Family Installments*

Russian

Berman, Chaim — *Patriarch*
Bullard, Arthur — *Comrade Yetta*
Tobenkin, Elias — *Witte Arrives*
Yezierska, Anzia — *How I Found America*

Scottish

Lofts, Nora — *Blossom Like a Rose*

Spanish

Forbes, Harrie — *Mission Tales in the Days of the Dons*

Swedish

Lindquist, Jennie — *Crystal Tree*

Nationality Abbreviations Used in the Indexes

Afr	African	**Ire**	Irish
Alb	Albanian	**It**	Italian
Arm	Armenian	**Jap**	Japanese
As	Asian	**Kor**	Korean
Aus	Australian	**Latv**	Latvian
Bah	Bahamian	**Leb**	Lebanese
Barb	Barbadian	**Lith**	Lithuanian
Bel	Belgian	**Mel**	Melanesian
Bur	Burmese	**Mex**	Mexican
Cam	Cambodian	**Nor**	Norwegian
Chil	Chilean	**Pak**	Pakistani
Chin	Chinese	**Peru**	Peruvian
Cro	Croatian	**Pol**	Polish
Cub	Cuban	**Port**	Portuguese
Cze	Czechoslovakian	**P R**	Puerto Rican
Dan	Danish	**Rus**	Russian
Dom	Dominican	**Scot**	Scottish
Dut	Dutch	**Sen**	Senegalese
Ecua	Ecuadoran	**Sp**	Spanish
El Sal	El Salvadoran	**Sw**	Swedish
Eng	English	**Tai**	Taiwanese
Euro	European	**Thai**	Thai
Fin	Finnish	**Trin**	Trinidadian
Fr	French	**Turk**	Turkish
Ger	German	**Ugan**	Ugandan
Gr	Greek	**Ukr**	Ukrainian
Guat	Guatemalan	**Viet**	Vietnamese
His	Hispanic	**W I**	West Indian
Hung	Hungarian	**Yug**	Yugoslavian
Ind	Indian		

Author Index

(References are to entry numbers and nationality abbreviations)

Adair, Margaret 147 *Fin*
Adams, Ruth J. 345 *Mex*
Addy, Sharon 97 *Cze*
Aiello, Barbara 206 *Gr*
Algren, Nelson 501 *Pol*
Allan, Mabel 230 *Ire*
Alvarez, Julia 110 *Dom*
Anaya, Rudolfo 346 *Mex,* 347 *Mex,* 348 *Mex*
Anderson, Eloise 215 *His*
Anderson, Joan 349 *Mex*
Anderson, Juanita 23 *Chin*
Anderson, Mary 222 *Hung,* 485 *Nor*
Anderson, Rachel 693 *Viet*
Andrews, Jean 499 *Pak*
Angell, Judie 602 *Rus*
Angelo, Valenti 255 *It*
Archer, Marion 486 *Nor*
Asch, Sholem 502 *Pol*
Ashabranner, Brent 694 *Viet*
Asher, Carol 166 *Ger*
Ashley, Bernard 24 *Chin*
Atkinson, Mary 350 *Mex*
Avi 125 *Eng*

Babbitt, Lorraine 351 *Mex*
Baker, Betty 167 *Ger*
Balch, Glenn 341 *Latv*
Bales, Carol Ann 25 *Chin*
Bang, Molly 283 *Jap*
Barker, Mary 98 *Cze*
Barrio, Edmond 352 *Mex*
Barth, Edna 527 *P R*
Battles, Edith 284 *Jap*
Beatty, Patricia 126 *Eng,* 353 *Mex*

Beckett, Hilary 354 *Mex,* 355 *Mex*
Behrens, June 26 *Chin,* 356 *Mex*
Beirne, Barbara 327 *Kor*
Belpre, Pura 528 *P R*
Benary-Isbert, Margot 168 *Ger*
Benasutti, Marion 256 *It*
Benezra, Barbara 27 *Chin*
Bennett, Jack 28 *Chin*
Berman, Chaim 603 *Rus*
Bernstein, Joanne 604 *Rus*
Betancourt, Jeanne 20 *Cam,* 328 *Kor,* 605 *Rus*
Bethancourt, T.E. 257 *It,* 357 *Mex,* 529 *P R,* 530 *P R*
Binzen, William 531 *P R,* 532 *P R*
Bishop, Curtis 90 *Cub,* 358 *Mex,* 359 *Mex*
Bloch, Marie 688 *Ukr*
Blue, Rose 360 *Mex,* 533 *P R,* 606 *Rus*
Bograd, Larry 361 *Mex*
Bojer, Johan 487 *Nor*
Bolognese, Don 362 *Mex*
Bolton, Carole 231 *Ire*
Bonham, Frank 285 *Jap,* 286 *Jap,* 363 *Mex,* 534 *P R*
Bonner, Louise 287 *Jap*
Bouchard, Lois 535 *P R*
Bourne, M. 536 *P R*
Bradford, Richard 216 *His*
Brandenberg, Aliki 207 *Gr*
Branson, Karen 232 *Ire,* 233 *Ire*
Breckenfeld, Vivian 288 *Jap*
Breckler, Rosemary 695 *Viet*
Breeding, Robert L. 127 *Eng*
Brenner, Barbara 364 *Mex,* 537 *P R*
Brown, Tricia 365 *Mex,* 696 *Viet*

111

AUTHOR INDEX

Bruni, Mary Ann 366 *Mex*
Buchan, Bryan 646 *Scot*
Buck, Pearl 29 *Chin*, 30 *Chin*
Budd, Lillian 661 *Sw*
Bulla, Clyde 128 *Eng*, 129 *Eng*, 367 *Mex*
Bullard, Arthur 607 *Rus*
Bunting, Eve 31 *Chin*
Burchard, Peter 538 *P R*
Burchardt, Nellie 539 *P R*
Burden-Patman, Denise 685 *Trin*
Burt, Katherine 503 *Pol*
Buss, Fran 124 *El Sal*
Bylinksy, Tatyana 258 *It*

Cahan, Abraham 608 *Rus*
Campion, Wardi 540 *P R*
Capron, Louis 647 *Scot*
Cardenas, Leo 368 *Mex*
Carlstrom, Nancy 217 *His*
Caseley, Judith 609 *Rus*
Cather, Willa 99 *Cze*, 488 *Nor*
Cavanna, Betty 289 *Jap*
Cebulash, Mel 697 *Viet*
Chang, Heidi 32 *Chin*, 33 *Chin*
Chao, Evelina 34 *Chin*
Charyn, Jerome 290 *Jap*
Chase, Mary 504 *Pol*
Chavez, Angelico 369 *Mex*
Chec, John 610 *Rus*
Cheng, Hou-Tien 35 *Chin*
Chessman, Ruth 130 *Eng*
Chetin, Helen 36 *Chin*
Chin, Frank 37 *Chin*
Choc, Sook Nyul 329 *Kor*
Christgau, Alice 662 *Sw*
Christman, Elizabeth 259 *It*
Christopher, Matt 223 *Hung*, 291 *Jap*, 541 *P R*, 611 *Rus*
Cisneros, Sandra 218 *His*, 370 *Mex*
Clark, Ann Nolan 148 *Fin*, 152 *Fr*, 371 *Mex*, 657 *Sp*
Clark, Margery 612 *Rus*
Clarke, Mary 131 *Eng*, 648 *Scot*
Coerr, Eleanor 38 *Chin*
Cofer, Judith 542 *P R*, 543 *P R*
Cohen, Barbara 613 *Rus*, 614 *Rus*
Colman, Hila 372 *Mex*, 544 *P R*, 615 *Rus*
Colver, Anne 169 *Ger*
Condon, Richard 234 *Ire*
Conlon-McKenna, Marita 235 *Ire*
Constiner, Merle 132 *Eng*
Cook, Bruce 373 *Mex*
Copeland, Helen 292 *Jap*
Coutant, Helen 698 *Viet*
Cox, William 91 *Cub*, 293 *Jap*, 374 *Mex*, 375 *Mex*, 376 *Mex*
Crane, Caroline 545 *P R*
Crayder, Dorothy 616 *Rus*
Crayer, Teresa 153 *Fr*
Cretan, Gladys 3 *Arm*, 4 *Arm*
Crew, Linda 21 *Cam*
Crompton, Anne 133 *Eng*
Cruz, Manuel 377 *Mex*
Cummings, Betty 236 *Ire*
Cummings, Rebecca 149 *Fin*
Curley, Daniel 237 *Ire*, 617 *Rus*

Dahl, Borghild 489 *Nor*, 490 *Nor*, 491 *Nor*
Danska, Herbert 546 *P R*
Dean, Karen 378 *Mex*
De Angeli, Marguerite 170 *Ger*
De Capite, Raymond 260 *It*, 261 *It*
De Jong, Dola 111 *Dut*
De Leon, Nephtali 379 *Mex*
De Mejo, Oscar 649 *Scot*
Diaz, Paul 380 *Mex*
Di Donato, Pietro 262 *It*, 263 *It*
Dionetti, Michelle 264 *It*
Dixon, Paige 699 *Viet*
Dolgin, P. 700 *Viet*
Drdek, Richard 100 *Cze*
Drizari, Nelo 2 *Alb*
Dunn, Marylois 701 *Viet*
Dunnahoo, Terry 361 *Mex*, 382 *Mex*, 383 *Mex*
Dunne, Mary 384 *Mex*

Edmonds, Walter 112 *Dut*
Embry, Margaret 385 *Mex*
Erdman, Loula 154 *Fr*
Ericson, Stig 663 *Sw*

AUTHOR INDEX

Estes, Eleanor 39 *Chin*, 505 *Pol*
Ets, Marie 386 *Mex*
Evans, Doris 40 *Chin*
Evernden, Margery 506 *Pol*

Fahrmann, Willi 171 *Ger*
Fall, Thomas 387 *Mex*
Farrar, Susan C. 618 *Rus*
Fast, Howard 172 *Ger,* 173 *Ger,* 174 *Ger*
Fenton, Edward 238 *Ire*
Fern, Eugene 219 *His*
Fernandez, Roberta 388 *Mex*
Field, Rachel 155 *Fr*
Fife, Dale 175 *Ger*
Figueroa, John 547 *P R*
Figueroa, Pablo 548 *P R*
Fine, Anne 619 *Rus*
Fineman, Irving 507 *Pol*
Fink, Augusta 389 *Mex*
Finlayson, Ann 134 *Eng*
Fisher, Leonard 239 *Ire,* 265 *It*
Fleischman, H. Samuel 549 *P R*
Fleming, Alice 176 *Ger*
Fletcher, David 266 *It*
Fletcher, Susan 177 *Ger*
Foley, June 208 *Gr*
Foltz, Mary Jane 524 *Port*
Forbes, Harrie 658 *Sp*
Forbes, Kathryn 492 *Nor*
Forgione, Louis 267 *It*
Forman, Marcey 620 *Rus*
Francis, Dorothy 686 *Turk*
Frazier, James 390 *Mex*
Freeman, Don 391 *Mex*
Friedman, Ina 294 *Jap*
Fulle, Suzanne 392 *Mex*

Galarza, Ernesto 393 *Mex*
Galbraith, Clare 394 *Mex*
Garcia, Guy 395 *Mex*
Garcia, Richard 550 *P R*
Garrison, Christian 295 *Jap*
Garthwaite, Marion 396 *Mex*
Gates, Doris 397 *Mex*
Gault, William 398 *Mex,* 551 *P R*

Gee, Maurice 399 *Mex*
Gelfand, Marilyn 621 *Rus*
George, Harry 209 *Gr*
Geras, Adele 622 *Rus*
Gerson, Corinne 400 *Mex*
Gibbs, Alonzo 113 *Dut*
Giff, Patricia 240 *Ire*
Gilson, Jamie 702 *Viet*
Godden, Rumer 689 *Ukr*
Gonzalez, Gloria 552 *P R*
Good, Merle 178 *Ger*
Goodwin, Harold 344 *Mel*
Granger, Peg 268 *It*
Gray, Genevieve 401 *Mex,* 553 *P R*
Gray, Patsey 402 *Mex*
Greene, Constance 403 *Mex*
Greene, Roberta 554 *P R*
Gregory, Diana 41 *Chin*
Griego, Jose 404 *Mex*
Griego, Maestas 404 *Mex*
Gross, Virginia 269 *It*
Gurasich, Marj 179 *Ger*
Guy, Rosa 715 *W I*

Hall, Lynn 555 *P R*
Hall, Marjory 135 *Eng*
Hamilton, Dorothy 405 *Mex*
Harris, Christie 136 *Eng,* 241 *Ire,* 650 *Scot*
Harvey, Brett 623 *Rus*
Haugaard, Erik 137 *Eng*
Haugaard, Kay 42 *Chin,* 296 *Jap*
Havill, Juanita 406 *Mex*
Hawkinson, Lucy 297 *Jap*
Hayes, Florence 298 *Jap*
Hays, Wilma 156 *Fr,* 651 *Scot*
Hearn, Emily 556 *P R*
Heller, Linda 624 *Rus*
Hernandez, Irene 407 *Mex*
Heuman, William 408 *Mex,* 557 *P R,* 558 *P R*
Hewett, Joan 409 *Mex,* 410 *Mex*
Hickman, Janet 101 *Cze,* 180 *Ger,* 181 *Ger*
Hinchman, Catherine 224 *Hung*
Hitte, Kathryn 411 *Mex*
Hodge, Jane 157 *Fr*
Hoff, Carol 182 *Ger*

Hoguet, Susan 138 *Eng*
Holland, Isabelle 92 *Cub*
Holman, Felice 220 *His,* 508 *Pol*
Hood, Flora 412 *Mex*
Hotze, Sollace 509 *Pol*
Houston, Jeanne 299 *Jap*
Howard, Ellen 43 *Chin*
Howe, John 114 *Dut*
Hoyt-Goldsmith, Diane 703 *Viet*
Hughes, Dean 682 *Tai*
Hunter, Evan 413 *Mex*
Hurwitz, Johanna 183 *Ger,* 559 *P R*

Inyart, Gene 300 *Jap*
Irving, Washington 115 *Dut*
Irwin, Hadley 242 *Ire,* 301 *Jap*
Irwin, Wallace 302 *Jap*
Ish-Kishor, Sul 139 *Eng*

Jackson, Jacqueline 158 *Fr,* 270 *It*
Janney, Russell 510 *Pol*
Janus, Christopher 210 *Gr*
Javernick, Ellen 9 *As*
Jaynes, Ruth 414 *Mex,* 415 *Mex,* 416 *Mex*
Jensen, Pauline 140 *Eng*
Johnson, Doris 330 *Kor*
Johnson, Lois W. 664 *Sw*
Jordan, Mildred 184 *Ger*

Kadohata, Cynthia 303 *Jap*
Kafka, Franz 102 *Cze*
Kanazawa, Tooru 304 *Jap*
Keating, Norma 44 *Chin*
Keats, Ezra 560 *P R*
Keehn, Sally 185 *Ger*
Keith, Harold 186 *Ger*
Kerle, Arthur 159 *Fr*
Kerr, Helen 108 *Dan*
Kerr, M.E. 187 *Ger*
Kesselman, Wendy 561 *P R*
Kherdian, David 5 *Arm,* 6 *Arm,* 7 *Arm*
Kingsolver, Barbara 214 *Guat*

Kingston, Maxine H. 45 *Chin*
Klein, Norma 160 *Fr*
Kline, Suzy 331 *Kor*
Konigsburg, E.L. 225 *Hung*
Kropp, Paul 687 *Ugan*
Krumgold, Joseph 144 *Euro,* 417 *Mex*
Kuklin, Susan 562 *P R,* 655 *Sen*
Kushner, Donn 511 *Pol*

Laklan, Carli 418 *Mex*
Lampman, Evelyn 419 *Mex,* 420 *Mex*
La Rouche, Adelle 46 *Chin*
Lasky, Kathryn 625 *Rus*
Lawson, Robert 243 *Ire*
Law-Yone, Wendy 19 *Bur*
Lee, Gus 47 *Chin*
Lee, Helen 48 *Chin*
Lee, Marie 332 *Kor,* 333 *Kor*
Lehmann, Linda 188 *Ger,* 189 *Ger*
Lehrman, Robert 626 *Rus*
Leighton, Maxinne 512 *Pol*
Lelchuk, Alan 627 *Rus*
L'Engle, Madeline 141 *Eng*
Lenski, Lois 49 *Chin,* 513 *Pol*
LeRoy, Gen 271 *It*
Levine, Ellen 50 *Chin*
Leviton, Sonia 190 *Ger*
Levoy, Myron 161 *Fr,* 191 *Ger,* 563 *P R*
Lewiton, Mina 226 *Hung,* 564 *P R,* 565 *P R*
Lexau, Joan 566 *P R,* 567 *P R*
Li, Chin-yang 51 *Chin*
Lim, Genny 52 *Chin*
Lindquist, Jennie 665 *Sw,* 666 *Sw,* 667 *Sw*
Line, David 227 *Hung*
Lo, Steven C. 53 *Chin*
Lofts, Nora 652 *Scot*
Lomas Garza, Carmen 421 *Mex*
Lord, Athena 211 *Gr,* 212 *Gr*
Lord, Bette 54 *Chin,* 55 *Chin*

McCabe, Inger 568 *P R*
McCunn, Ruthanne 56 *Chin,* 57 *Chin*

McDaniel, Becky B. 10 *As,* 11 *As,* 12 *As*
McDonald, Joyce 334 *Kor*
McGiffin, Lee 659 *Sp*
McLerran, Alice 628 *Rus*
MacMillan, Dianne 335 *Kor,* 422 *Mex,* 704 *Viet*
Madison, Winifred 423 *Mex*
Maguire, Gregory 629 *Rus*
Mangione, Jerre 272 *It*
Mann, Peggy 569 *P R,* 570 *P R,* 571 *P R,* 572 *P R*
Mannix, Daniel 192 *Ger*
Marangell, Virginia 273 *It*
Mark, Michael 514 *Pol*
Marshall, Paule 17 *Barb*
Martel, Cruz 573 *P R*
Martin, Ann 705 *Viet*
Martin, Patricia 58 *Chin,* 424 *Mex*
Marvin, Isabel 425 *Mex*
Marzollo, Jean 426 *Mex*
Maury, Inez 427 *Mex,* 428 *Mex*
Mays, Lucinda 274 *It*
Means, Florence 429 *Mex,* 574 *P R*
Melendez, Carmello 575 *P R*
Miklowitz, Gloria 305 *Jap*
Miles, Betty 275 *It*
Milhous, Katherine 116 *Dut*
Miller, Helen 150 *Fin*
Mills, Claudia 93 *Cub*
Mills, Donia 430 *Mex*
Mitchell, Barbara 103 *Cze,* 117 *Dut*
Moberg, Vilhelm 668 *Sw,* 669 *Sw*
Mohr, Nicholasa 576 *P R,* 577 *P R,* 578 *P R,* 579 *P R,* 580 *P R*
Molarsky, Osmond 22 *Chil*
Molloy, Anne 500 *Peru*
Molnar, Joe 59 *Chin,* 431 *Mex,* 581 *P R*
Monjo, F.N. 118 *Dut*
Moore, Ruth 104 *Cze,* 105 *Cze,* 106 *Cze,* 582 *P R,* 706 *Viet*
Mora, Pat 432 *Mex*
Moskin, Marietta 119 *Dut,* 630 *Rus*
Mukherjee, Bharati 229 *Ind*
Murphy, Barbara 162 *Fr*
Murray, Michelle 193 *Ger*

Namioka, Lensey 60 *Chin,* 61 *Chin*
Nathan, Dorothy 631 *Rus*
Newman, Shirlee P. 62 *Chin,* 525 *Port*
Niemeyer, Marie 63 *Chin*
Nixon, Joan 244 *Ire,* 632 *Rus*
Norris, Gunella 670 *Sw*

O'Connor, Edwin 245 *Ire,* 246 *Ire*
O'Dell, Scott 213 *Gr,* 433 *Mex,* 434 *Mex,* 656 *Sen*
Ogan, Margaret 435 *Mex*
Okada, John 306 *Jap*
Okimoto, Jean 307 *Jap*
Olsen, Violet 109 *Dan*
Ormsby, Virginia 436 *Mex,* 437 *Mex*

Paek, Min 336 *Kor*
Pagano, Jo 276 *It*
Panetta, George 277 *It*
Papashvily, George 633 *Rus*
Paredes, Americo 438 *Mex*
Parini, Jay 278 *It*
Parker, Richard 498 *Pak*
Pascal, Francine 64 *Chin*
Paterson, Katherine 707 *Viet*
Patton, Willoughby 526 *Port*
Paul, Louis 279 *It*
Paul, Paula 439 *Mex*
Paulsen, Gary 440 *Mex,* 493 *Nor*
Peck, Robert 163 *Fr*
Pellegrini, Nina 337 *Kor*
Pellowski, Anne 515 *Pol,* 516 *Pol,* 517 *Pol,* 518 *Pol,* 519 *Pol*
Perez, Norah 247 *Ire*
Pesera, Hilda 94 *Cub*
Phipson, Joan 13 *Aus*
Pinkwater, Daniel 65 *Chin*
Place, Marian 441 *Mex*
Plummer, Louise 120 *Dut*
Polacco, Patricia 634 *Rus,* 635 *Rus,* 636 *Rus,* 690 *Ukr*
Politi, Leo 66 *Chin,* 67 *Chin,* 308 *Jap,* 442 *Mex,* 443 *Mex,* 444 *Mex,* 445 *Mex,* 446 *Mex,* 447 *Mex*

AUTHOR INDEX

Polovchak, Walter 691 *Ukr*
Ponce, Mary 448 *Mex*
Price, Eugenia 660 *Sp*
Prieto, Mariana 16 *Bah,* 95 *Cub,* 449 *Mex,* 583 *P R*
Pundt, Helen 164 *Fr*

Reed, Fran 450 *Mex*
Reiff, Tana 68 *Chin,* 96 *Cub,* 145 *Euro,* 165 *Fr,* 194 *Ger,* 248 *Ire,* 280 *It,* 281 *It,* 451 *Mex,* 494 *Nor,* 708 *Viet,* 709 *Viet*
Reit, Seymour 69 *Chin,* 584 *P R*
Rivera, Edward 585 *P R*
Rivera, Tomas 452 *Mex*
Roberts, Cecil 520 *Pol*
Robertson, Keith 70 *Chin*
Roe, Eileen 453 *Mex*
Roldan, Fernando 454 *Mex*
Rolvaag, Ole 495 *Nor,* 496 *Nor,* 497 *Nor*
Rose, Anne 18 *Bel*
Roseman, Kenneth 637 *Rus*
Rosenberg, Liz 146 *Euro*
Rosenberg, Maxine 338 *Kor*
Rowe, Jack 249 *Ire*
Rowland, Florence 195 *Ger*
Roy, Cal 455 *Mex*
Ruby, Lois 71 *Chin*

Sachs, Marilyn 586 *P R,* 638 *Rus*
St. George, Judith 121 *Dut*
Sandin, Joan 671 *Sw,* 672 *Sw*
Santiago, Danny 456 *Mex*
Savin, Marcia 309 *Jap*
Sawyer, Ruth 250 *Ire,* 282 *It*
Say, Allen 72 *Chin*
Scarboro, Elizabeth 683 *Tai*
Schaefer, Jack 457 *Mex*
Schellie, Don 458 *Mex*
Schoberle, Cecile 459 *Mex*
Selz, Irma 196 *Ger*
Sendak, Philip 521 *Pol*
Shapiro, Irwin 717 *Yug*
Shaw, Janet 673 *Sw,* 674 *Sw,* 675 *Sw,* 676 *Sw,* 677 *Sw,* 678 *Sw*

Shearer, J. 587 *P R*
Shefelman, Janice 197 *Ger,* 198 *Ger,* 342 *Leb*
Sherman, Eileen 639 *Rus*
Shiefman, Vicky 640 *Rus*
Shotwell, Louisa 588 *P R,* 589 *P R*
Shura, Mary 251 *Ire*
Shyer, Marlene 590 *P R*
Sinclair, Upton 343 *Lith*
Sinykin, Sheri 339 *Kor*
Skurzynski, Gloria 107 *Cze,* 692 *Ukr*
Sleater, William 684 *Thai*
Smith, Doris 310 *Jap*
Smith, Mary Lou 460 *Mex*
Sobol, Harriet 340 *Kor*
Solbert, Ronnie 591 *P R*
Sonneborn, Ruth 592 *P R,* 593 *P R,* 594 *P R*
Soto, Gary 461 *Mex,* 462 *Mex,* 463 *Mex*
Speevack, Yetta 595 *P R*
Spicer, Dorothy 122 *Dut*
Stanek, Muriel 464 *Mex*
Steinbeck, John 465 *Mex*
Sterne, Emma 1 *Afr*
Stock, Catherine 73 *Chin*
Stolz, Mary 252 *Ire*
Strange, Celia 466 *Mex*
Sugimoto, E.I. 311 *Jap*
Summers, James 467 *Mex,* 468 *Mex*
Surat, Michele 710 *Viet*

Taha, Karen 469 *Mex*
Talbot, Charlene 253 *Ire,* 596 *P R*
Talbot, Toby 597 *P R*
Tamar, Erika 228 *Hung*
Tan, Amy 74 *Chin,* 75 *Chin*
Tashjian, Virginia 8 *Arm*
Taylor, Mark 312 *Jap*
Taylor, Theodore 470 *Mex*
Telemaque, Eleanor 76 *Chin*
Terris, Susan 77 *Chin*
Texter, Sylvia 471 *Mex*
Thaler, Susan 598 *P R*
Thomas, Dawn 599 *P R,* 600 *P R*
Tobenkin, Elias 199 *Ger,* 641 *Rus*
Tolstoy, Leo 642 *Rus*

AUTHOR INDEX

Tran, Kim-Lan 711 *Viet*
Tran-Khanh-Tuyet 712 *Viet*
Trivelpiece, Laurel 472 *Mex*
Turner, Ann Warren 713 *Viet*
Turngren, Ellen 679 *Sw*

Uchida, Yoshiko 313 *Jap*, 314 *Jap*, 315 *Jap*, 316 *Jap*, 317 *Jap*, 318 *Jap*, 319 *Jap*, 320 *Jap*, 321 *Jap*, 322 *Jap*, 323 *Jap*

Van Der Veer, Judy 473 *Mex*
Vasquez, Richard 474 *Mex*
Villarreal, Jose 475 *Mex*
Vineberg, Ethel 643 *Rus*

Wainwright, Richard 123 *Ecua*
Walley, Constance 200 *Ger*
Warren, Mary 476 *Mex*
Wartski, Maureen 714 *Viet*
Waters, Kate 78 *Chin*
Waterton, Betty 522 *Pol*
Watson, Sally 653 *Scot*
Weaver, Robert 201 *Ger*
Weik, Mary 202 *Ger*
Weiman, Eiveen 203 *Ger*
Weiner, Sandra 601 *P R*
Weiss, Nicki 221 *His*

Weller, Frances 654 *Scot*
White, Edgar 716 *W I*
Whitney, Phyllis 477 *Mex*
Wiberg, Harold 680 *Sw*
Wier, Ester 14 *Aus*
Williams, Jeanne 644 *Rus*
Williams, Vera 478 *Mex*, 479 *Mex*, 480 *Mex*, 481 *Mex*
Williamson, Joanne 142 *Eng*, 204 *Ger*
Winter, Jeanette 681 *Sw*
Wisler, G. Clifton 143 *Eng*
Wisniowski, Sygurd 523 *Pol*
Withey, Barbara 205 *Ger*
Wolf, Bernard 482 *Mex*
Wong, Jade Snow 79 *Chin*
Wong, Shawn 80 *Chin*
Worchester, Gurdon 151 *Fin*
Wrightson, Patricia 15 *Aus*
Wyndham, Robert 81 *Chin*

Yashima, Mitsu 324 *Jap*
Yashima, Taro 325 *Jap*
Yates, Elizabeth 254 *Ire*
Yee, Paul 82 *Chin*
Yep, Laurence 83 *Chin*, 84 *Chin*, 85 *Chin*, 86 *Chin*, 87 *Chin*, 88 *Chin*
Yezierska, Anzia 645 *Rus*
Yoshida, Jim 326 *Jap*
Young, Alida 89 *Chin*
Young, Bob 483 *Mex*, 484 *Mex*

Title Index

(References are to entry numbers and nationality abbreviations)

Absolutely Perfect Horse 701 *Viet*
Across the Great River 407 *Mex*
Across the Sea from Galway 239 *Ire*
Across the Tracks 483 *Mex*
Adam Bookout 588 *P R*
Aekyung's Dream 336 *Kor*
After the Picnic 268 *It*
Alan and Naomi 161 *Fr*
Alexandra 213 *Gr*
All Except Sammy 3 *Alb*
All This Wild Land 148 *Fin*
Amanda's Choice 92 *Cub*
American Scrapbook 290 *Jap*
Amerika 102 *Cze*
Ameryka 100 Years Old 523 *Pol*
Amish Wedding 195 *Ger*
And Forever Free 204 *Ger*
...And Now Miguel 417 *Mex*
And the Earth Did Not Devour Him 452 *Mex*
Angel Child, Dragon Child 710 *Viet*
Angel Island Prisoner 36 *Chin*
Angelita 561 *P R*
Anita's Choice 405 *Mex*
Antonio's World 547 *P R*
Apple Pie and Onions 609 *Rus*
April Harvest 661 *Sw*
Around Another Corner 556 *P R*
Asking the River 5 *Alb*

Backfield Challenge 551 *P R*
Bad Boy, Good Boy 386 *Mex*
Bandit of Mok Hill 419 *Mex*
Barrio Boy 393 *Mex*
Barto Takes the Subway 537 *P R*

Baseball Flyhawk 541 *P R*
Baseball in April 461 *Mex*
Bean Trees 214 *Guat*
Before the Wild Flowers Bloom 258 *It*
Benito 367 *Mex*
Best Bad Thing 313 *Jap*
Betsy's Up-and-Down Year 515 *Pol*
Better Than a Princess 188 *Ger*
Billy Beg and the Bull 237 *Ire*
Binkey and the Bamboo Brush 046 *Chin*
Birthday Basket for Tia 432 *Mex*
Birthday Visitor 314 *Jap*
Bizou 160 *Fr*
Bless Me, Ultima 346 *Mex*
Blossom Like a Rose 652 *Scot*
Blue Willow 397 *Mex*
Boat of Longing 495 *Nor*
Boat People 708 *Viet*
Boat Song 654 *Scot*
Bound for Freedom 130 *Eng*
Boy in the 49th Seat 298 *Jap*
Boy Who Wasn't Lonely 499 *Pak*
Boy Who Wouldn't Talk 535 *P R*
Brandywine 249 *Ire*
Bread and Butter Indian 169 *Ger*
Bridge of Friendship 230 *Ire*
Brown Girl, Brownstones 17 *Barb*
Buddy Trap 339 *Kor*
Burma Rifles 285 *Jap*
By Marvelous Agreement 111 *Dut*

Calico Bush 155 *Fr*
Call Me Ruth 638 *Rus*

TITLE INDEX

Candita's Choice 564 *P R*
Cargo 344 *Mel*
Carlos Goes to School 215 *His*
Carly and Co. 697 *Viet*
Carmen 531 *P R*
Carnival 685 *Trin*
Casa Means Home 540 *P R*
Castle on Hester Street 624 *Rus*
Cathy and Lisette 153 *Fr*
Chair for My Mother 478 *Mex*
Changes for Kirsten 673 *Sw*
Chang's Paper Pony 38 *Chin*
Charley Yee's New Year 23 *Chin*
Charlie's House 128 *Eng*
Chicano 474 *Mex*
Chicano, Amigo 399 *Mex*
Chicano Christmas Story 377 *Mex*
Chicano Cruz 374 *Mex*
Chicano Girl 372 *Mex*
Chicken by Che 165 *Fr*
Child of Fire 433 *Mex*
Child of the Owl 83 *Chin*
Children of the River 21 *Cam*
China Boy 42 *Chin*
China Boy 47 *Chin*
Chinatown Sunday 25 *Chin*
Chinese Children Next Door 29 *Chin*
Chinese New Year 35 *Chin*
Chinese Story Teller 30 *Chin*
Chito 535 *P R*
Christ in Concrete 262 *It*
Christmas at the Tomten's Farm 680 *Sw*
Christmas Surprise 104 *Cze*
City High Champion 557 *P R*
City High Five 408 *Mex*
Class President 559 *P R*
Cleversticks 24 *Chin*
Clubhouse 569 *P R*
Coal Mine Peaches 264 *It*
Coffin Tree 19 *Bur*
Cold Rain on the Water 606 *Rus*
Coming of Fabrizze 260 *It*
Comrade Yetta 607 *Rus*
Copper Sunrise 646 *Scot*
Crystal Nights 193 *Ger*
Crystal Tree 665 *Sw*
Cuban Boy's Adventures in America 94 *Cub*

Cuentos: Tales from the Hispanic Southwest 404 *Mex*

Dan Henry in the Wild West 663 *Sw*
Dance, Dance, Amy-Chan 297 *Jap*
Danza 555 *P R*
Dark Side of Nowhere 553 *P R*
Daughter of the Moon 629 *Rus*
Daughter of the Samurai 311 *Jap*
Day Luis Was Lost 527 *P R*
Dear Uncle Carlos 584 *P R*
Demo of 70th Street 209 *Gr*
Different Ball Game 22 *Chil*
Different Home 96 *Cub*
Distant Thunder 105 *Cze*
Dmitry: A Young Soviet Immigrant 604 *Rus*
Don Juan McQueen 660 *Sp*
Donald Duk 37 *Chin*
Don't Come Back a Stranger 467 *Mex*
Don't Look at Me That Way 545 *P R*
Door Is Open 280 *It*
Dragonwings 84 *Chin*
Dream Eater 295 *Jap*
Dream Keeper 506 *Pol*
Dream with Storms 450 *Mex*
Duffy's Rock 238 *Ire*
Dunderhead War 167 *Ger*
During Water Peaches 472 *Mex*

Edge of Sadness 245 *Ire*
Egg Tree 116 *Dut*
Eggs: Greek Folk Tale 207 *Gr*
El Bronx Remembered 576 *P R*
El Chino 72 *Chin*
Elaine and the Flying Frog 32 *Chin*
Elaine, Mary Lewis, and the Frogs 33 *Chin*
Elizabeth 581 *P R*
Elizabeth and the Young Stranger 226 *Hung*
Ellis Island Christmas 512 *Pol*
Emigrants 487 *Nor*

TITLE INDEX

Emigrants 668 *Sw*
Emilio's Summer Day 536 *P R*
Emma's Dragon Hunt 73 *Chin*
Enrique 548 *P R*
Esmeralda and the Pet Parade 459 *Mex*

Fair Play 687 *Ugan*
Falling in Love Is No Snap 208 *Gr*
Families Are Different 337 *Kor*
Family from Vietnam 709 *Viet*
Family Installments 585 *P R*
Family Pictures 421 *Mex*
Famous All Over Town 456 *Mex*
Far Voice Calling 147 *Fin*
Farewell to Manzanar 299 *Jap*
Farolitos of Christmas 347 *Mex*
Fast Break 358 *Mex*
Fawn 163 *Fr*
Feast of Light 670 *Sw*
Feast on Sullivan Street 275 *It*
Felita 577 *P R*
Fidelia 345 *Mex*
Fields Breathe Sweet 113 *Dut*
Fiesta! 356 *Mex*
Fifth Chinese Daughter 79 *Chin*
Finding My Voice 332 *Kor*
Fire Dragon 27 *Chin*
First Farm in the Valley: Anna's Story 516 *Pol*
First Snow 698 *Viet*
Flag Is Up 402 *Mex*
Floating World 303 *Jap*
Flood 166 *Ger*
For Gold and Blood 68 *Chin*
Forbidden Frontier 241 *Ire*, 650 *Scot*
Forty-Niners 649 *Scot*
Foster Mary 466 *Mex*
Four Seas to Dreamland 2 *Alb*
Fourth Grade Dinosaur Club 361 *Mex*
Freedom's Child 691 *Ukr*
Friday Night Is Papa Night 592 *P R*
Friday Surprise 391 *Mex*
Friends 715 *W I*
From London to Appalachia 127 *Eng*

Game 100 *Cze*
Game, Set and Match 91 *Cub*
Gang Girl 549 *P R*
Gates of Grace 34 *Chin*
Gaucho 552 *P R*
George Washington Gomez 438 *Mex*
Gianna Mia 273 *It*
Gift for Tia Rose 469 *Mex*
Gift of the Pirate Queen 240 *Ire*
Girl from Puerto Rico 544 *P R*
Girl from Two Miles High 500 *Peru*
Glorious Conspiracy 142 *Eng*
Go Up the Road 420 *Mex*
Going Home 578 *P R*
Golden Gate 255 *It*
Golden Name Day 666 *Sw*
Golden Wedding 276 *It*
Good News 489 *Nor*
Good-bye, Amigos 484 *Mex*
Good-bye Billy Radish 692 *Ukr*
Goodbye to the Trees 640 *Rus*
Gooseberries to Oranges 613 *Rus*
Graciela 431 *Mex*
Grandma's Gun 424 *Mex*
Grandmother and the Runaway Shadow 146 *Euro*
Grandmother Came from Dworitz 643 *Rus*
Grandmother's Adobe Dollhouse 460 *Mex*
Granny Project 619 *Rus*
Great Wheel 243 *Ire*
Greenhorn on the Frontier 134 *Eng*

Halmoni 329 *Kor*
Hanukkah of Great-Uncle Otto 191 *Ger*
Happiest Ending 315 *Jap*
Happy as the Grass Was Green 178 *Ger*
Happy Birthday, Kirsten! 674 *Sw*
Happy Funeral 31 *Chin*
Healer 192 *Ger*
Hear, Ye Sons 507 *Pol*
Heart of Aztlan 348 *Mex*
Hearts Are the Fields 679 *Sw*

TITLE INDEX

Hector Lives in the United States Now 409 *Mex*
Helga's Magic 108 *Dan*
Hello, Amigos! 365 *Mex*
Hello, My Name Is Scrambled Eggs 702 *Viet*
Her Own Song 43 *Chin*
Highland Halloween 651 *Scot*
Hilarion 617 *Rus*
Him She Loves? 187 *Ger*
Hoang Anh: Vietnamese-American 703 *Viet*
Hoang Breaks the Lucky Teapot 695 *Viet*
Hold the Rein Free 473 *Mex*
Home and Home Again 633 *Rus*
Home Sweet Home 605 *Rus*
Homebase 80 *Chin*
Homecoming 490 *Nor*
Hornet's Nest 653 *Scot*
Horrible Harry's Secret 331 *Kor*
Hotheads 271 *It*
House of Conrad 199 *Ger*
House on Liberty Street 202 *Ger*
House on Mango Street 218 *His*
How Far, Felipe? 401 *Mex*
How I Found America 645 *Rus*
How Juan Got Home 570 *P R*
How My Family Lives in America 562 *P R*, 655 *Sen*
How My Parents Learned to Eat 294 *Jap*
How the Garcia Girls Lost Their Accents 110 *Dom*
Hue and Cry 254 *Ire*
Hundred Dresses 505 *Pol*
Hungry No More 248 *Ire*

I Am Here: Yo Estoy Agui 533 *P R*
I Am Regina 185 *Ger*
I Hate English! 50 *Chin*
I Speak English for My Mom 464 *Mex*
I Will Catch the Sun 379 *Mex*
I Wrote My Name on the Wall 591 *P R*
Ice Trail 133 *Eng*

If It Hadn't Been for Yoon Jun 333 *Kor*
Immigrant Girl 623 *Rus*
Immigrants 173 *Ger*
Immigrant's Daughter 172 *Ger*
In Grandpa's House 521 *Pol*
In Nueva York 579 *P R*
In the Year of the Boar and Jackie Robinson 54 *Chin*
In This Proud Land 482 *Mex*
Incorporation of Eric Chung 53 *Chin*
Independence Avenue 639 *Rus*
Intaglio 388 *Mex*
Into a Strange Land 694 *Viet*
Iron Peacock 131 *Eng*, 648 *Scot*
It Happened at Cecilia's 228 *Hung*
It's Crazy to Stay Chinese in Minnesota 76 *Chin*
It's Only Goodbye 269 *It*

Jar of Dreams 316 *Jap*
Jenny 300 *Jap*
Jenny Kimura 289 *Jap*
Joe Magarac and His U.S.A. Citizenship Papers 717 *Yug*
Johnny Lost 95 *Cub*
Johnny Texas 182 *Ger*
Joker and the Swan 616 *Rus*
Josefina and the Hanging Tree 425 *Mex*
Jose's Christmas Secret 566 *P R*
Journey Home 317 *Jap*
Journey of the Sparrows 124 *El S*
Journey to Boston 504 *Pol*
Journey to Topaz 318 *Jap*
Joy Luck Club 74 *Chin*
Juanita 442 *Mex*
Juan's 18 Wheeler Summer 441 *Mex*
Jungle 343 *Lith*

Kaisa Kilponen: Two Stories 149 *Fin*
Kathleen, Please Come Home 434 *Mex*

TITLE INDEX

Katie Can 10 *As*
Katie Couldn't 11 *As*
Katie Did It 12 *As*
Katy, Be Good 196 *Ger*
Keeping Quilt 634 *Rus*
Kim/Kimi 242 *Ire*, 301 *Jap*
King of Prussia and a Peanut Butter Sandwich 176 *Ger*
King's Goblet 266 *It*
Kirsten Learns a Lesson 675 *Sw*
Kirsten Saves the Day 676 *Sw*
Kirsten's Surprise 677 *Sw*
Kirsti 150 *Fin*
Kitchen God's Wife 75 *Chin*
Kitchen Madonna 689 *Ukr*
Kite 454 *Mex*
Klara's New World 681 *Sw*

Land of Hope 632 *Rus*
Land of Promise 244 *Ire*
Land of the Golden Mountain 51 *Chin*
Land of the Iron Dragon 89 *Chin*
Lanterns for Fiesta 392 *Mex*
Last Hurrah 246 *Ire*
Latchkey Kids 77 *Chin*
Laugh at the Evil Eye 686 *Turk*
Laura Loves Horses 410 *Mex*
Lee Ann 696 *Viet*
Letters from Italy 265 *It*
Letters of a Japanese Schoolboy 302 *Jap*
Letters to Oma 179 *Ger*
Light: Story of a Small Kindness 217 *His*
Line of the Sun 542 *P R*
Lion and the Puppy 642 *Rus*
Lion Dancer: Ernie Wan's Chinese New Year 78 *Chin*
Lion to Guard Us 129 *Eng*
Little Fear 15 *Aus*
Little Italy 281 *It*
Little League Amigo 90 *Cub*
Little League Double Play 359 *Mex*
Little League Hotshots 558 *P R*
Little Man in the Family 587 *P R*
Little Silver House 667 *Sw*

Little Weaver of Thai-Yen Village 712 *Viet*
Lollipop Party 593 *P R*
Long Black Schooner 1 *Afr*
Long Journey of Lucas B. 171 *Ger*
Long Time Coming 477 *Mex*
Long Time Growing 575 *P R*
Long Way from Home 714 *Viet*
Long Way Home 168 *Ger*
Long Way Home from Troy 430 *Mex*
Long Way to a New Land 671 *Sw*
Long Way Westward 672 *Sw*
Lok Who's Playing First Base 611 *Rus*
Los Posadas 390 *Mex*
Lost King 261 *It*
Lost Umbrella of Kim Chu 39 *Chin*
Luck of Z.A.P. and Zoe 211 *Gr*
Luisa's American Dream 93 *Cub*
Lupita Manana 353 *Mex*
Lysbet and the Fire Kittens 119 *Dut*

Magdalena 589 *P R*
Magic Paper 451 *Mex*
Mail-Order Kid 334 *Kor*
Maldonado Miracle 470 *Mex*
Mama's Bank Account 492 *Nor*
Manuel, Young Mexican American 403 *Mex*
Manuel's Discovery 526 *Port*
Maria 567 *P R*
Maria Luisa 423 *Mex*
Maria Teresa 350 *Mex*
Mariana 378 *Mex*
Mario 396 *Mex*
Marya of Clark Avenue 688 *Ukr*
Masks, a Love Story 28 *Chin*
Matchlock Gun 112 *Dut*
Maybe Next Summer 458 *Mex*
Me Inside of Me 357 *Mex*
Meet Kirsten, an American Girl 678 *Sw*
Meet Miki Takino 292 *Jap*
Melinda's Christmas Stocking 414 *Mex*
Melting Pot 637 *Rus*
Mexicali Soup 411 *Mex*

TITLE INDEX

Mexican Standoff 373 *Mex*
Mieko 308 *Jap*
Migrant Girl 418 *Mex*
Miguel's Mountain 532 *P R*
Mik and the Prowler 319 *Jap*
Mile High 234 *Ire*
Milenka's Happy Summer 98 *Cze*
Mira! Mira! 599 *P R*
Miracle of the Bells 510 *Pol*
Miss Fourth of July, Goodbye 210 *Gr*
Mission Bell 443 *Mex*
Mission Tales in the Days of the Dons 658 *Sp*
Mr. Charley's Chopsticks 40 *Chin*
Mr. Chu 44 *Chin*
Mr. Fong's Toy Shop 66 *Chin*
Molly by Any Other Name 307 *Jap*
Molly's Pilgrim 614 *Rus*
Momo's Kitten 324 *Jap*
Moon Bridge 309 *Jap*
Moon Guitar 63 *Chin*
More Than Meets the Eye 20 *Cam*, 328 *Kor*
Mother 502 *Pol*
Mount Allegro 272 *It*
Mountains to Climb 123 *Ecua*
Moy Moy 67 *Chin*
Murderer 508 *Pol*
Music, Music for Everyone 479 *Mex*
My Ántonia 99 *Cze*
My Aunt Otilia's Spirits 550 *P R*
My Best Friend, Duc Tran 704 *Viet*
My Best Friend, Martha Rodriguez 422 *Mex*
My Best Friend, Mee-Yung 335 *Kor*
My Brother, Angel 354 *Mex*
My Dog Is Lost! 560 *P R*
My Friend Leslie 338 *Kor*
My Grandfather and Me 48 *Chin*
My Grandmother's Journey 610 *Rus*
My Great-Grandpa Joe 621 *Rus*
My House Is Your House 597 *P R*
My Mother and I Are Growing Strong 427 *Mex*
My Mother the Mail Carrier 428 *Mex*
My Name Is Not Angelica 656 *Sen*
Myeko's Gift 296 *Jap*

Mystery in Little Tokyo 286 *Jap*
Mystery of the Disappearing Dogs 364 *Mex*
Mystery of the Fat Cat 534 *P R*
Mystery of the Missing Stallions 706 *Viet*

Neon Wilderness 501 *Pol*
New Day 362 *Mex*
New York City, Too Far from Tampa Blues 257 *It*, 529 *P R*
Nice Guy, Go Home 201 *Ger*
Nice Italian Girl 259 *It*
Nicest Gift 444 *Mex*
Nicolau's Prize 524 *Port*
Night Journey 625 *Rus*
Nilda 580 *P R*
No-No Boy 306 *Jap*
No Steady Job for Papa 256 *It*
Noonday Friends 252 *Ire*
Now, Ameriky 236 *Ire*

O Little Town 194 *Ger*
O Pioneers! 488 *Nor*
Obstinate Land 186 *Ger*
Oh, Brother! 400 *Mex*
Old Fasnacht 117 *Dut*
Old Ramon 457 *Mex*
Old Ways, New Ways 145 *Euro*
On a Hot, Hot Day 221 *His*
On Home Ground 627 *Rus*
Once I Was a Plum Tree 183 *Ger*
Once There Was and Was Not 8 *Arm*
One Another 162 *Fr*
One Boy at a Time 41 *Chin*
One Luminaria for Antonia 412 *Mex*
One Small Candle 520 *Pol*
One-way to Ansonia 602 *Rus*
Onion John 144 *Euro*
Open Gate: New Year's 1815 156 *Fr*
Orphan for Nebraska 253 *Ire*
Orphans of the Wind 137 *Eng*
Other Girl 135 *Eng*
Other Shore 274 *It*

TITLE INDEX

Other Side of the Sun 141 *Eng*
Our Eddie 139 *Eng*
Out of Reach 64 *Chin*
Owl's Nest 122 *Dut*

Pablito's New Feet 600 *P R*
Paco's Miracle 152 *FR*, 371 *Mex*
Papa Luigi's Marionettes 279 *It*
Paper Crane 283 *Jap*
Paradise Called Texas 197 *Ger*
Park's Quest 707 *Viet*
Passage 247 *Ire*
Patch Boys 278 *It*
Patriarch 603 *Rus*
Peace Treaty 106 *Cze*
Peddler's Dream 342 *Leb*
Pedro, Angel of Olvera Street 445 *Mex*
Peg-Leg Willy 385 *Mex*
Pepito's Story 219 *His*
Petranella 522 *Pol*
Pianist's Debut 327 *Kor*
Picture Bride 320 *Jap*
Pie-Biter 56 *Chin*
Pink Like the Geranium 351 *Mex*
Play Off 682 *Tai*
Plum Plum Pickers 352 *Mex*
Pocho 475 *Mex*
Poppy Seed Cakes 612 *Rus*
Portrait of Me 206 *Gr*
Potato Eaters 232 *Ire*
Promised Year 321 *Jap*
Promises to Keep 699 *Viet*
Proud to Be Amish 184 *Ger*
Push to the West 494 *Nor*

Queen's Own Grove 126 *Eng*

Rachel's Legacy 615 *Rus*
Rafael and the Raiders 355 *Mex*
Rainbow People 85 *Chin*
Reach Out, Ricardo 384 *Mex*
Rechenka's Eggs 690 *Ukr*

Red Sky at Morning 216 *His*
Red War Pole 647 *Scot*
Refugee 18 *Bel*
Return to Ramos 368 *Mex*
Rice Bowl Pet 58 *Chin*
Rice Cakes and Paper Dragons 69 *Chin*
Riders of Enchanted Valley 659 *Sp*
Rip Van Winkle 114 *Dut*
Rip Van Winkle and the Legend of Sleepy Hollow 115 *Dut*
Rise of David Levinsky 608 *Rus*
River Between 267 *It*
Road from Home: Story of an Armenian Girl 6 *Arm*
Roller Skates 250 *Ire*, 282 *It*
Romantic Obsessions and Humiliations of Annie Sehlmeier 120 *Dut*
Room to Grow 154 *Fr*
Rooster That Understood Japanese 322 *Jap*
Rosaria 598 *P R*
Roses Sing on New Snow 82 *Chin*
Rosita's Christmas Wish 366 *Mex*
Rudi and the Distelfink 118 *Dut*
Rumptydoolers 14 *Aus*
Runaway to Glory 662 *Sw*
Runaways 341 *Latv*
Russian in the Attic 620 *Rus*

Salted Lemons 310 *Jap*
Samantha on Stage 618 *Rus*
Samurai of Gold Hill 323 *Jap*
San Francisco Boy 49 *Chin*
Santiago 528 *P R*
Sati, the Rastafarian 716 *W I*
Savannah Purchase 157 *Fr*
Sea Glass 86 *Chin*
Search of Mary Katherine Mulloy 231 *Ire*
Second Generation 174 *Ger*
Secret City, U.S.A. 220 *His*
Secret in the Dorm Attic 498 *Pak*
Secret Language of the SB 683 *Tai*
Secrets 628 *Rus*
Sentries 440 *Mex*
Serpent and the Sun 455 *Mex*
Serpent Ring 205 *Ger*

TITLE INDEX

Serpent's Children 87 *Chin*
Seven in Bed 594 *P R*
Shad Are Running 121 *Dut*
Shadow Like a Leopard 563 *P R*
Shadow of the Valley 476 *Mex*
Sherman 59 *Chin*
Shipwrecked Dog 525 *Port*
Shoe Full of Shamrock 251 *Ire*
Shoeshine Boys 277 *It*
Short Stories of Fray Angelico Chavez 369 *Mex*
Shortstop from Tokyo 291 *Jap*
Shy One 631 *Rus*
Silent Dancing 543 *P R*
Silver Days 190 *Ger*
Singing Flute 151 *Fin*
Six Generations 200 *Ger*
Skin Deep 395 *Mex*
Skippack School 170 *Ger*
Skirt 462 *Mex*
Soccer Sam 426 *Mex*
Soldier and Me 227 *Hung*
Solomon Grundy 138 *Eng*
Something Special for Me 480 *Mex*
Song for the Swallows 446 *Mex*
Song for Uncle Harry 7 *Arm*
Soo Ling Finds a Way 26 *Chin*
Spanish Pioneers of the Southwest 349 *Mex*
Spider Plant 595 *P R*
Spirit House 684 *Thai*
Spirit of Iron 198 *Ger*
Spring Comes First to the Willows 164 *Fr*
Spring Moon 55 *Chin*
Stairstep Farm: Anna Rose's Story 517 *Pol*
Star Fisher 88 *Chin*
Stones 180 *Ger*
Store That Mama Built 626 *Rus*
Street Kids 546 *P R*
Street of the Flower Boxes 571 *P R*
Streets of Gold 233 *Ire*
Stringbean's Trip to the Shining Sea 481 *Mex*
Strong Citadel 508 *Pol*
Stuttgart Nanny Mafia 177 *Ger*
SuAn 330 *Kor*
Sumatra Alley 132 *Eng*
Summer Endings 509 *Pol*

Sunday for Sona 4 *Arm*
Surprise for Carlotta 539 *P R*
Sushi and Sourdough 304 *Jap*

Taking Sides 463 *Mex*
Tales the People Tell in China 81 *Chin*
Taste of Spruce Gum 158 *Fr,* 270 *It*
Tell Me Please, What's That 415 *Mex*
Tempering 107 *Cze*
Tennis Bum 435 *Mex*
Tet: The New Year 711 *Viet*
That Bad Carlos 565 *P R*
That's Not My Style 222 *Hung*
Their Father's God 496 *Nor*
There Is a Happy Land 486 *Nor*
They Call Me Jack 601 *P R*
Thicker Than Water 140 *Eng*
Third and Goal 375 *Mex*
Third Life of Per Smevik 497 *Nor*
This Is Espie Sanchez 381 *Mex*
This New Land 143 *Eng*
This Old Man 71 *Chin*
Thousand Pieces of Gold 57 *Chin*
Three Circles in Light 263 *It*
Three Stalks of Corn 447 *Mex*
Through Moon and Stars and Night Skies 713 *Viet*
Throwing Shadows 225 *Hung*
Thunder Cake 635 *Rus*
Tiger's Daughter 229 *Ind*
Tilli's New World 189 *Ger*
Time for Flowers 312 *Jap*
Tino 590 *P R*
To Touch the Sky 389 *Mex*
Toba at the Hands of a Thief 514 *Pol*
Today's Special Z.A.P. and Zoe 212 *Gr*
Tomahawks and Trombones 103 *Cze*
Tomas and the Talking Birds 582 *P R*
Tomas Takes Charge 596 *P R*
Tomato Boy 16 *Bah,* 583 *P R*
Torchlight 224 *Hung*

TITLE INDEX

Tortilla Flat 465 *Mex*
Treasure Nap 406 *Mex*
Trouble at Second 398 *Mex*
Trouble at Second Base 293 *Jap*, 376 *Mex*
Trouble at Wild River 664 *Sw*
True Confessions of Charlotte Doyle 125 *Eng*
Truth About Mary Rose 586 *P R*
Twenty-one Children Plus Ten 436 *Mex*
21 Mile Swim 223 *Hung*
Two and Me Makes Three 554 *P R*
Two Worlds of Jim Yoshida 326 *Jap*
Two Worlds of Noriko 288 *Jap*

Uncle Jacob's Ghost Story 511 *Pol*
Uncle Vova's Tree 636 *Rus*
Under This Roof 491 *Nor*
Unto a Good Land 669 *Sw*
Up from El Paso 380 *Mex*
Us Maltbys 429 *Mex*, 574 *P R*

Valley of the Shadow 101 *Cze*
Victor 394 *Mex*
View from the Pighouse Roof 109 *Dan*
Visit with Great-Grandma 97 *Cze*
Viva Chicano 363 *Mex*
Voyage 622 *Rus*

Waiting for Mama 630 *Rus*
Walk a Narrow Bridge 175 *Ger*
Walk Proud 413 *Mex*
War Between the Classes 305 *Jap*
War Orphan 693 *Viet*
We Are Chicano 360 *Mex*
We Don't Look Like Our Mom and Dad 340 *Kor*
We Laughed a Lot, My First Day of School 471 *Mex*
We Live in the North 513 *Pol*
Wedding 448 *Mex*

Week in Henry's World 568 *P R*
West with the White Chiefs 136 *Eng*
What Does the Rooster Say, Yoshio? 284 *Jap*
What Is a Birthday Child 416 *Mex*
What's My Name in Hawaii? 287 *Jap*
What's Wrong with Julio? 437 *Mex*
When Carlos Closed the Street 572 *P R*
When the City Stopped 13 *Aus*
When the Monkeys Wore Sombreros 449 *Mex*
Where the Deer and the Cantaloupe Play 530 *P R*
Where's Brooke 9 *As*
Which Way Courage? 203 *Ger*
Whispering Trees 159 *Fr*
Who Cares About Espie Sanchez? 382 *Mex*
Who Needs Espie Sanchez? 383 *Mex*
Who Says Nobody's Perfect? 485 *Nor*
Who's Hu? 60 *Chin*
Wild Boy 387 *Mex*
Wildflower Girl 235 *Ire*
Willow Wind Farm: Betsy's Story 518 *Pol*
Winding Valley Farm: Annie's Story 519 *Pol*
Wingman 65 *Chin*
Wings for Lai Ho 52 *Chin*
Winter Room 493 *Nor*
Winter Wheat 644 *Rus*
With My Brother (Con mi Hermano) 453 *Mex*
Witte Arrives 641 *Rus*
Woman Hollering Creek 370 *Mex*
Woman Warrior 45 *Chin*

Yagua Days 573 *P R*
Yang the Youngest and His Terrible Ear 61 *Chin*
Year of the Jeep 70 *Chin*
Year Walk 657 *Sp*
Yellow Silk for May Lee 62 *Chin*

Yin's Special Thanksgiving 700 *Viet*
You Can Hear a Magpie Smile 439 *Mex*
You Can't Make It by Bus 468 *Mex*

Youngest One 325 *Jap*
Yours Truly, Shirley 705 *Viet*

Zoar Blue 181 *Ger*

Subject Index

(References are to entry numbers and nationality abbreviations)

Adoption 43 *Chin,* 242 *Ire,* 301 *Jap,* 307 *Jap,* 330 *Kor,* 333 *Kor,* 334 *Kor,* 337 *Kor,* 340 *Kor,* 713 *Viet; see also* Orphans
Adventure 65 *Chin,* 95 *Cub,* 123 *Ecua,* 160 *Fr,* 171 *Ger,* 204 *Ger,* 214 *Guat,* 454 *Mex,* 465 *Mex,* 481 *Mex,* 527 *P R,* 649 *Scot*
African Americans 476 *Mex*
Alcohol Abuse 383 *Mex*
Americans in Other Countries 266 *It*
Animals/Donkeys 401 *Mex*
Animals/Fox 334 *Kor*
Animals/Goats 459 *Mex*
Animals/Llamas 123 *Ecua*
Animals/Sheep 14 *Aus,* 417 *Mex,* 457 *Mex*
Animals/Zoo 415 *Mex; see also* Cats; Dogs; Horses, Trained; Horses, Wild
Arts & Artists 3 *Arm,* 58 *Chin,* 367 *Mex,* 505 *Pol,* 563 *P R*

Babysitting 108 *Dan,* 177 *Ger*
Ballet 64 *Chin,* 378 *Mex,* 616 *Rus,* 618 *Rus; see also* Dancing
Biography, Fictionalized 2 *Alb,* 418 *Mex,* 585 *P R,* 521 *Pol,* 57 *Chin,* 72 *Chin,* 79 *Chin,* 240 *Ire,* 326 *Jap*
Birds 443 *Mex*
Birthdays 314 *Jap,* 365 *Mex,* 416 *Mex,* 422 *Mex,* 432 *Mex,* 442 *Mex,* 480 *Mex,* 584 *P R,* 674 *Sw*
Blindness 123 *Ecua,* 535 *P R*
Boats & Boating 4 *Arm*

Boys, Mature 107 *Cze,* 132 *Eng,* 204 *Ger,* 243 *Ire,* 306 *Jap,* 435 *Mex,* 452 *Mex,* 458 *Mex,* 530 *P R*
Boys, Pre-teen 22 *Chil,* 61 *Chin,* 94 *Cub,* 95 *Cub,* 170 *Ger,* 209 *Gr,* 262 *It,* 269 *It,* 287 *Jap,* 371 *Mex,* 396 *Mex,* 399 *Mex,* 409 *Mex,* 417 *Mex,* 453 *Mex,* 471 *Mex,* 524 *Port,* 527 *P R,* 532 *P R,* 536 *P R,* 556 *P R,* 569 *P R,* 582 *P R,* 588 *P R,* 599 *P R,* 601 *P R,* 612 *Rus,* 620 *Rus,* 683 *Tai,* 702 *Viet,* 703 *Viet*
Boys, Teen 5 *Arm,* 14 *Aus,* 46 *Chin,* 70 *Chin,* 100 *Cze,* 101 *Cze,* 211 *Gr,* 228 *Hung,* 263 *It,* 354 *Mex,* 363 *Mex,* 419 *Mex,* 440 *Mex,* 504 *Pol,* 535 *P R,* 570 *P R,* 575 *P R,* 585 *P R,* 587 *P R,* 604 *Rus,* 639 *Rus,* 699 *Viet*
Brothers 68 *Chin,* 278 *It,* 449 *Mex,* 453 *Mex,* 481 *Mex,* 659 *Sp,* 672 *Sw; see also* Brothers & Sisters; Siblings
Brothers & Sisters 19 *Bur,* 154 *Fr,* 210 *Gr,* 211 *Gr,* 212 *Gr,* 244 *Ire,* 252 *Ire,* 354 *Mex,* 537 *P R,* 596 *P R,* 619 *Rus,* 673 *Sw,* 706 *Viet; see also* Brothers; Siblings; Sisters
Burma 285 *Jap*

Canada 136 *Eng*
Captivities 106 *Cze,* 133 *Eng,* 185 *Ger,* 198 *Ger*
Careers 96 *Cub,* 165 *Fr,* 172 *Ger,* 234 *Ire,* 267 *It,* 280 *It,* 342 *Leb,* 380 *Mex,* 395 *Mex,* 418 *Mex,* 575 *P R,* 608 *Rus; see also* Working World

SUBJECT INDEX

Cats 119 *Dut*, 321 *Jap*, 324 *Jap*
Cherokee 127 *Eng*
China 30 *Chin*, 75 *Chin*, 87 *Chin*
Citizenship 149 *Fin*, 194 *Ger*, 287 *Jap*, 304 *Jap*, 451 *Mex*, 717 *Yug*
Civil Rights 201 *Ger*
Civil War, American 137 *Eng*, 181 *Ger*
Classics 115 *Dut*, 343 *Lith*, 465 *Mex*
Clothing & Dress 62 *Chin,* 371 *Mex,* 462 *Mex*
College 259 *It*, 467 *Mex*, 641 *Rus*
Colonial America 127 *Eng,* 131 *Eng*, 135 *Eng*, 648 *Scot*, 653 *Scot*
Community Life 48 *Chin*, 49 *Chin*, 60 *Chin*, 200 *Ger*, 238 *Ire*, 260 *It*, 261 *It*, 263 *It*, 281 *It*, 295 *Jap*, 326 *Jap*, 346 *Mex*, 362 *Mex*, 408 *Mex*, 421 *Mex*, 489 *Nor*, 553 *P R*, 560 *P R*, 569 *P R*, 571 *P R*, 577 *P R*, 588 *P R*, 591 *P R*, 595 *P R*, 597 *P R*, 696 *Viet*; see also Daily Life; Lifestyle
Courage 75 *Chin*, 112 *Dut*, 121 *Dut*, 387 *Mex*, 441 *Mex*, 701 *Viet*, 714 *Viet*
Crime 15 *Aus*, 383 *Mex*, 395 *Mex*, 588 *P R*, 662 *Sw*
Cultural Conflict 163 *Fr*, 164 *Fr*, 175 *Ger*, 182 *Ger*, 206 *Gr*, 249 *Ire*, 293 *Jap*, 311 *Jap*, 332 *Kor*, 336 *Kor*, 368 *Mex*, 376 *Mex*, 490 *Nor*, 686 *Turk*, 708 *Viet*; see also Cultural Differences; Cultural Traits
Cultural Differences 22 *Chil*, 50 *Chin*, 60 *Chin*, 78 *Chin*, 79 *Chin*, 80 *Chin*, 93 *Cub*, 102 *Cze*, 140 *Eng*, 145 *Euro*, 154 *Fr*, 179 *Ger*, 199 *Ger*, 202 *Ger*, 255 *It*, 296 *Jap*, 300 *Jap*, 302 *Jap*, 323 *Jap*, 326 *Jap*, 337 *Kor*, 344 *Mel*, 488 *Nor*, 497 *Nor*, 526 *Port*, 542 *P R*, 562 *P R*, 601 *P R*, 605 *Rus*, 646 *Scot*, 655 *Sen*, 688 *Ukr*, 703 *Viet*; see also Cultural Conflict; Cultural Traits
Cultural Traits 24 *Chin*, 37 *Chin*, 40 *Chin*, 41 *Chin*, 47 *Chin*, 108 *Dan*, 114 *Dut*, 116 *Dut*, 209 *Gr*, 212 *Gr*, 223 *Hung*, 225 *Hung*, 242 *Ire*, 276 *It*, 294 *Jap*, 297 *Jap*, 300 *Jap*, 301 *Jap*, 308 *Jap*, 315 *Jap*, 347 *Mex*, 425 *Mex*, 455 *Mex*, 460 *Mex*, 513 *Pol*, 628 *Rus*, 667 *Sw*, 669 *Sw*, 685 *Trin*, 693 *Viet*, 695 *Viet*; see also Cultural Differences; Cultural Conflicts
Customs 81 *Chin*, 107 *Cze*, 122 *Dut*, 184 *Ger*

Daily Life 8 *Arm*, 25 *Chin*, 29 *Chin*, 49 *Chin*, 58 *Chin*, 138 *Eng*, 156 *Fr*, 197 *Ger*, 489 *Nor*, 507 *Pol*, 587 *P R*, 601 *P R*, 623 *Rus*; see also Lifestyle; Community Life
Dancing 462 *Mex*
Deafness 254 *Ire*, 499 *Pak*
Death 31 *Chin*, 139 *Eng*, 698 *Viet*
Decisions 409 *Mex*, 627 *Rus*, 637 *Rus*
Delaware Indians 103 *Cze*, 185 *Ger*
Delinquency 363 *Mex*, 598 *P R*
Depression Era 109 *Dan*, 232 *Ire*, 313 *Jap*, 316 *Jap*, 475 *Mex*, 508 *Pol*, 615 *Rus*
Description 660 *Sp*
Detective 373 *Mex*
Dogs 364 *Mex*, 444 *Mex*, 560 *P R*, 525 *Port*
Dolls 188 *Ger*, 567 *P R*
Dreams 295 *Jap*, 406 *Mex*
Drug Abuse 373 *Mex*, 413 *Mex*

Earthquake 27 *Chin*, 399 *Mex*
Elderly 15 *Aus*, 144 *Euro*, 180 *Ger*, 213 *Gr*, 346 *Mex*, 457 *Mex*, 469 *Mex*
England 227 *Hung*
Escapes 133 *Eng*, 393 *Mex*

Family 2 *Alb*, 7 *Arm*, 17 *Barb*, 25 *Chin*, 27 *Chin*, 34 *Chin*, 55 *Chin*, 59 *Chin*, 63 *Chin*, 69 *Chin*, 77 *Chin*, 80 *Chin*, 87 *Chin*, 96 *Cub*,

100 *Cze*, 139 *Eng*, 140 *Eng*, 141 *Eng*, 143 *Eng*, 168 *Ger*, 172 *Ger*, 173 *Ger*, 186 *Ger*, 190 *Ger*, 191 *Ger*, 194 *Ger*, 199 *Ger*, 224 *Hung*, 232 *Ire*, 238 *Ire*, 239 *Ire*, 245 *Ire*, 248 *Ire*, 251 *Ire*, 258 *It*, 264 *It*, 267 *It*, 273 *It*, 276 *It*, 281 *It*, 290 *Jap*, 292 *Jap*, 303 *Jap*, 304 *Jap*, 317 *Jap*, 318 *Jap*, 320 *Jap*, 321 *Jap*, 335 *Kor*, 336 *Kor*, 340 *Kor*, 342 *Leb*, 349 *Mex*, 353 *Mex*, 362 *Mex*, 365 *Mex*, 370 *Mex*, 375 *Mex*, 386 *Mex*, 393 *Mex*, 397 *Mex*, 404 *Mex*, 406 *Mex*, 411 *Mex*, 414 *Mex*, 421 *Mex*, 431 *Mex*, 432 *Mex*, 438 *Mex*, 469 *Mex*, 474 *Mex*, 478 *Mex*, 479 *Mex*, 480 *Mex*, 486 *Nor*, 487 *Nor*, 488 *Nor*, 491 *Nor*, 492 *Nor*, 495 *Nor*, 501 *Pol*, 504 *Pol*, 509 *Pol*, 511 *Pol*, 515 *Pol*, 539 *P R*, 545 *P R*, 548 *P R*, 550 *P R*, 553 *P R*, 562 *P R*, 568 *P R,* 573 *P R*, 576 *P R*, 578 *P R*, 581 *P R*, 584 *P R*, 586 *P R*, 592 *P R*, 594 *P R*, 599 *P R*, 600 *P R*, 603 *Rus*, 604 *Rus*, 606 *Rus*, 612 *Rus*, 622 *Rus*, 625 *Rus*, 626 *Rus*, 631 *Rus*, 633 *Rus*, 634 *Rus*, 636 *Rus*, 639 *Rus*, 640 *Rus*, 655 *Sen*, 662 *Sw*, 665 *Sw*, 668 *Sw*, 669 *Sw*, 671 *Sw*, 672 *Sw*, 678 *Sw*, 681 *Sw*, 684 *Thai*, 689 *Ukr*, 691 *Ukr*, 704 *Viet*, 709 *Viet*
Famine 231 *Ire*, 232 *Ire*, 239 *Ire*, 247 *Ire*
Fantasy 65 *Chin*, 251 *Ire*, 283 *Jap*
Fathers 509 *Pol*, 654 *Scot*; *see also* Fathers & Daughters; Fathers & Sons
Fathers & Daughters 9 *As*, 43 *Chin*, 83 *Chin*, 110 *Dom*, 174 *Ger*, 244 *Ire*, 613 *Rus*; *see also* Fathers
Fathers & Sons 84 *Chin*, 86 *Chin*, 171 *Ger*, 265 *It*, 269 *It*, 323 *Jap*, 344 *Mel*, 391 *Mex*, 627 *Rus*, 707 *Viet*, 711 *Viet*; *see also* Fathers
Fears 235 *Ire*, 538 *P R*, 635 *Rus*
Festivals 35 *Chin*, 286 *Jap*, 297 *Jap*, 308 *Jap*, 371 *Mex*, 442 *Mex*
Fish and Fishing 121 *Dut*, 708 *Viet*

Flood 42 *Chin*, 411 *Mex*
Folklore 56 *Chin*, 73 *Chin*, 85 *Chin*, 207 *Gr*, 446 *Mex*; *see also* Legends
Food 40 *Chin*, 82 *Chin*, 447 *Mex*, 612 *Rus*, 700 *Viet*
Foster Care 94 *Cub*, 288 *Jap*, 429 *Mex*, 466 *Mex*, 574 *P R*, 683 *Tai*, 694 *Viet*
Friendship 7 *Arm*, 16 *Bah*, 71 *Chin*, 92 *Cub*, 134 *Eng*, 144 *Euro*, 161 *Fr*, 169 *Ger*, 216 *His*, 219 *His*, 230 *Ire*, 252 *Ire*, 298 *Jap*, 309 *Jap*, 310 *Jap*, 325 *Jap*, 331 *Kor*, 338 *Kor*, 352 *Mex*, 386 *Mex*, 397 *Mex*, 400 *Mex*, 422 *Mex*, 467 *Mex*, 498 *Pak*, 546 *P R*, 554 *P R*, 561 *P R*, 583 *P R*, 628 *Rus*, 646 *Scot*, 700 *Viet*; *see also* Friendship Among Boys; Friendship Among Girls
Friendship Among Boys 90 *Cub*, 358 *Mex*, 359 *Mex*, 361 *Mex*, 399 *Mex*, 415 *Mex*, 663 *Sw*, 704 *Viet*; *see also* Friendship
Friendship Among Girls 32 *Chin*, 33 *Chin*, 153 *Fr*, 198 *Ger*, 226 *Hung*, 531 *P R*, 618 *Rus*, 675 *Sw*, 715 *W I*; *see also* Friendship
Frontier Life 134 *Eng*, 148 *Fin*, 167 *Ger*, 186 *Ger*, 657 *Sp*, 663 *Sw*, 673 *Sw*, 674 *Sw*, 675 *Sw*, 676 *Sw*, 677 *Sw*, 678 *Sw*

Games 9 *As*, 591 *P R*
Gangs 413 *Mex*, 433 *Mex*, 456 *Mex*, 468 *Mex*, 530 *P R*, 549 *P R*, 563 *P R*, 572 *P R*
Generation Gap 26 *Chin*, 55 *Chin*, 63 *Chin*, 271 *It*, 329 *Kor*, 487 *Nor*, 490 *Nor*, 589 *P R*, 679 *Sw*, 691 *Ukr*
Ghosts 511 *Pol*, 550 *P R*, 684 *Thai*
Gifts 377 *Mex*, 432 *Mex*, 592 *P R*
Girls, Mature 51 *Chin*, 113 *Dut*, 203 *Ger*, 214 *Guat*, 224 *Hung*, 231 *Ire*, 256 *It*, 510 *Pol*, 661 *Sw*
Girls, Pre-teen 10 *As*, 11 *As*, 12 *As*,

SUBJECT INDEX

18 *Bel*, 39 *Chin*, 62 *Chin*, 119 *Dut*, 177 *Ger*, 205 *Ger*, 250 *Ire*, 282 *It*, 308 *Jap*, 309 *Jap*, 314 *Jap*, 321 *Jap*, 431 *Mex*, 439 *Mex*, 469 *Mex*, 500 *Peru*, 522 *Pol*, 539 *P R*, 584 *P R*, 586 *P R*, 670 *Sw*, 676 *Sw*, 688 *Ukr*, 696 *Viet*
Girls, Teen 6 *Arm*, 17 *Barb*, 36 *Chin*, 52 *Chin*, 60 *Chin*, 71 *Chin*, 77 *Chin*, 82 *Chin*, 88 *Chin*, 99 *Cze*, 126 *Eng*, 160 *Fr*, 164 *Fr*, 166 *Ger*, 175 *Ger*, 179 *Ger*, 185 *Ger*, 188 *Ger*, 189 *Ger*, 193 *Ger*, 235 *Ire*, 241 *Ire*, 244 *Ire*, 313 *Jap*, 332 *Kor*, 336 *Kor*, 368 *Mex*, 378 *Mex*, 381 *Mex*, 382 *Mex*, 383 *Mex*, 392 *Mex*, 405 *Mex*, 407 *Mex*, 472 *Mex*, 476 *Mex*, 483 *Mex*, 485 *Nor*, 503 *Pol*, 515 *Pol*, 516 *Pol*, 517 *Pol*, 518 *Pol*, 519 *Pol*, 543 *P R*, 544 *P R*, 549 *P R*, 578 *P R*, 581 *P R*, 589 *P R*, 598 *P R*, 605 *Rus*, 616 *Rus*, 640 *Rus*, 650 *Scot*, 666 *Sw*, 686 *Turk*
Grandparents 26 *Chin*, 30 *Chin*, 31 *Chin*, 46 *Chin*, 48 *Chin*, 73 *Chin*, 83 *Chin*, 97 *Cze*, 98 *Cze*, 117 *Dut*, 146 *Euro*, 264 *It*, 312 *Jap*, 329 *Kor*, 351 *Mex*, 402 *Mex*, 500 *Peru*, 506 *Pol*, 609 *Rus*, 610 *Rus*, 619 *Rus*, 621 *Rus*, 625 *Rus*, 635 *Rus*, 698 *Viet*
Gypsies 205 *Ger*

Handicapped 266 *It*, 705 *Viet*
Handicrafts 116 *Dut*, 356 *Mex*, 690 *Ukr*, 712 *Viet*
Health & Medicine 439 *Mex*, 600 *P R*, 692 *Ukr*
Historical Fiction 132 *Eng*, 142 *Eng*, 246 *Ire*, 297 *Jap*, 419 *Mex*, 602 *Rus*
Holidays 23 *Chin*, 35 *Chin*, 44 *Chin*, 66 *Chin*, 67 *Chin*, 69 *Chin*, 78 *Chin*, 104 *Cze*, 108 *Dan*, 191 *Ger*, 275 *It*, 335 *Kor*, 347 *Mex*, 356 *Mex*, 366 *Mex*, 377 *Mex*, 390 *Mex*, 412 *Mex*, 414 *Mex*, 442 *Mex*, 444 *Mex*, 445 *Mex*, 512 *Pol*, 566 *P R*, 636 *Rus*, 651 *Scot*, 677 *Sw*, 680 *Sw*, 685 *Trin*, 688 *Ukr*, 690 *Ukr*, 711 *Viet*
Horses, Trained 38 *Chin*, 341 *Latv*, 402 *Mex*, 410 *Mex*, 473 *Mex*, 555 *P R*, 701 *Viet*
Horses, Wild 387 *Mex*
Housing 460 *Mex*
Humorous 53 *Chin*, 56 *Chin*, 114 *Dut*, 115 *Dut*, 228 *Hung*, 234 *Ire*, 294 *Jap*, 385 *Mex*, 449 *Mex*, 459 *Mex*, 572 *P R*, 585 *P R*, 590 *P R*, 624 *Rus*, 717 *Yug*

Illness (diabetes) 206 *Gr*
Industrial Revolution 142 *Eng*
Internment Camps 290 *Jap*, 299 *Jap*, 318 *Jap*, 320 *Jap*
Irish 301 *Jap*
Island Life 526 *Port*

Japanese 242 *Ire*
Jealousy 485 *Nor*, 616 *Rus*
Jews 18 *Bel*, 139 *Eng*, 145 *Euro*, 183 *Ger*, 187 *Ger*, 193 *Ger*, 230 *Ire*, 502 *Pol*, 508 *Pol*, 514 *Pol*, 614 *Rus*, 615 *Rus*, 622 *Rus*, 623 *Rus*, 625 *Rus*, 630 *Rus*, 634 *Rus*, 637 *Rus*, 641 *Rus*, 643 *Rus*, 645 *Rus*
Journalism 173 *Ger*, 204 *Ger*, 458 *Mex*, 641 *Rus*
Justice 241 *Ire*, 254 *Ire*, 363 *Mex*, 650 *Scot*

Kidnapping 169 *Ger*
Kites 454 *Mex*, 547 *P R*

Land Ownership 389 *Mex*
Language Differences 284 *Jap*, 394 *Mex*, 415 *Mex*, 464 *Mex*, 533 *P R*, 535 *P R,* 570 *P R*, 582 *P R*

Leadership 348 *Mex*, 559 *P R*
Legends 237 *Ire*, 404 *Mex*, 447 *Mex*; *see also* Folklore
Lifestyle 8 *Arm*, 45 *Chin*, 74 *Chin*, 84 *Chin*, 118 *Dut*, 155 *Fr*, 196 *Ger*, 200 *Ger*, 349 *Mex*, 403 *Mex*, 667 *Sw*
Lonesomeness 32 *Chin*, 98 *Cze*, 436 *Mex*, 437 *Mex*, 523 *Pol*, 525 *Port*, 558 *P R,* 710 *Viet*, 716 *W I*
Loyalty 16 *Bah*, 21 *Cam*, 152 *Fr*, 306 *Jap*, 403 *Mex*, 439 *Mex*, 463 *Mex*, 583 *P R*, 629 *Rus*, 712 *Viet*

Marine Mammals 86 *Chin*, 147 *Fin*
Marriage 195 *Ger*, 448 *Mex*, 496 *Nor*
Mennonites 176 *Ger*
Mental Illness 161 *Fr*
Migrant Workers 352 *Mex*, 360 *Mex*, 380 *Mex*, 384 *Mex*, 392 *Mex*, 397 *Mex,* 405 *Mex*, 420 *Mex*, 431 *Mex*, 450 *Mex*, 466 *Mex*, 470 *Mex*, 475 *Mex*, 477 *Mex*, 482 *Mex*, 484 *Mex*
Mines & Mining 51 *Chin*, 649 *Scot*
Mohawk 163 *Fr*
Moneymaking 16 *Bah*, 70 *Chin*, 312 *Jap*, 552 *P R*
Moravians 101 *Cze*, 103 *Cze*, 104 *Cze*, 105 *Cze*
Mothers 630 *Rus*; *see also* Mothers & Daughters; Mothers & Sons
Mothers & Daughters 74 *Chin*, 148 *Fin*, 188 *Ger*, 427 *Mex*, 428 *Mex*, 434 *Mex*, 462 *Mex*, 464 *Mex*, 502 *Pol*, 638 *Rus*, 667 *Sw*; *see also* Mothers
Mothers & Sons 552 *P R*, 566 *P R*; *see also* Mothers
Murder 125 *Eng*, 227 *Hung*
Music 3 *Arm*, 151 *Fin*, 257 *It*, 327 *Kor*, 339 *Kor*, 345 *Mex*, 479 *Mex*, 520 *Pol,* 529 *P R*, 591 *P R*, 654 *Scot*
Mystery 39 *Chin*, 63 *Chin*, 151 *Fin*, 286 *Jap*, 319 *Jap*, 355 *Mex*, 364 *Mex*, 395 *Mex*, 499 *Pak*, 534 *P R*, 548 *P R*, 664 *Sw*, 697 *Viet*, 706 *Viet*

Names 287 *Jap*, 666 *Sw*
Native Americans 389 *Mex*, 443 *Mex*, 646 *Scot*

Ojibwa 159 *Fr*
Orphans 44 *Chin*, 111 *Dut*, 253 *Ire*, 367 *Mex*, 694 *Viet*, 712 *Viet*; *see also* Adoption

Physically Handicapped 338 *Kor*, 600 *P R*, 652 *Scot*
Pilgrims 143 *Eng*
Plants 522 *Pol*
Play 532 *P R*, 536 *P R*, 599 *P R*
Political Issues 52 *Chin*, 246 *Ire*, 343 *Lith*
Poultry 322 *Jap*, 385 *Mex*, 528 *P R*, 590 *P R*
Poverty 19 *Bur*, 189 *Ger*, 220 *His*, 236 *Ire*, 252 *Ire*, 317 *Jap*, 353 *Mex*, 407 *Mex*, 412 *Mex*, 433 *Mex*, 478 *Mex*, 482 *Mex*, 505 *Pol*, 568 *P R*, 579 *P R*, 580 *P R*
Pregnancy 259 *It*, 448 *Mex*
Prejudice 20 *Cam*, 28 *Chin*, 88 *Chin*, 89 *Chin*, 91 *Cub*, 136 *Eng*, 190 *Ger*, 208 *Gr*, 236 *Ire*, 268 *It*, 271 *It*, 274 *It*, 289 *Jap*, 291 *Jap*, 303 *Jap*, 316 *Jap*, 328 *Kor*, 361 *Mex*, 372 *Mex*, 374 *Mex*, 379 *Mex*, 396 *Mex*, 398 *Mex*, 423 *Mex*, 429 *Mex*, 438 *Mex*, 474 *Mex*, 476 *Mex*, 477 *Mex*, 508 *Pol*, 544 *P R*, 551 *P R*, 574 *P R*, 577 *P R*, 580 *P R*, 661 *Sw*, 687 *Ugan*, 699 *Viet*, 714 *Viet*
Puppets 66 *Chin*, 279 *It*, 350 *Mex*

Quakers 135 *Eng*

Railroads 68 *Chin*, 89 *Chin*
Refugees 157 *Fr*
Religion 25 *Chin*, 101 *Cze*, 105 *Cze*, 106 *Cze*, 113 *Dut*, 163 *Fr*, 176 *Ger*, 178 *Ger*, 183 *Ger*, 184 *Ger*, 195 *Ger*, 196 *Ger*, 201 *Ger*, 203 *Ger*, 245 *Ire*, 272 *It*, 369 *Mex*, 443 *Mex*, 445 *Mex*, 470 *Mex*, 496 *Nor*
Responsibility 99 *Cze*, 240 *Ire*, 324 *Jap*, 417 *Mex*
Romance 21 *Cam*, 28 *Chin*, 41 *Chin*, 64 *Chin*, 76 *Chin*, 93 *Cub*, 135 *Eng*, 150 *Fin*, 153 *Fr*, 162 *Fr*, 187 *Ger*, 208 *Gr*, 229 *Ind*, 249 *Ire*, 256 *It*, 259 *It*, 268 *It*, 288 *Jap*, 305 *Jap*, 307 *Jap*, 315 *Jap*, 320 *Jap*, 430 *Mex*, 468 *Mex*, 472 *Mex*, 474 *Mex*, 510 *Pol*, 520 *Pol*, 629 *Rus*, 652 *Scot*
Runaways 181 *Ger*, 341 *Latv*, 382 *Mex*, 434 *Mex*, 620 *Rus*
Rural Life 14 *Aus*, 109 *Dan*, 113 *Dut*, 369 *Mex*, 493 *Nor*, 494 *Nor*, 497 *Nor*, 516 *Pol*, 517 *Pol*, 518 *Pol*, 519 *Pol*, 542 *P R*, 659 *Sp*

School 20 *Cam*, 24 *Chin*, 32 *Chin*, 50 *Chin*, 54 *Chin*, 59 *Chin*, 120 *Dut*, 170 *Ger*, 215 *His*, 229 *Ind*, 272 *It*, 296 *Jap*, 298 *Jap*, 305 *Jap*, 328 *Kor*, 331 *Kor*, 333 *Kor*, 350 *Mex*, 351 *Mex*, 360 *Mex*, 379 *Mex*, 391 *Mex*, 394 *Mex*, 430 *Mex*, 436 *Mex*, 437 *Mex*, 450 *Mex*, 471 *Mex*, 533 *P R*, 557 *P R*, 559 *P R*, 564 *P R*, 581 *P R*, 614 *Rus*, 670 *Sw*, 702 *Viet*, 710 *Viet*
Scottish 241 *Ire*
Self-Esteem 5 *Arm*, 339 *Kor*, 538 *P R*, 595 *P R*, 631 *Rus*, 654 *Scot*, 707 *Viet*
Seminole 647 *Scot*
Sex Education 278 *It*
Ships 125 *Eng*, 137 *Eng*, 247 *Ire*
Short Stories 85 *Chin*, 149 *Fin*, 217 *His*, 218 *His*, 225 *Hung*, 440 *Mex*, 455 *Mex*, 461 *Mex*, 501 *Pol*, 513 *Pol*, 543 *P R*, 576 *P R*, 579 *P R*, 642 *Rus*, 645 *Rus*, 658 *Sp*
Siblings 10 *As*, 11 *As*, 12 *As*, 124 *El Sal*, 129 *Eng*, 345 *Mex*, 705 *Viet*, 715 *W I*; *see also* Brothers; Brothers & Sisters; Sisters
Sisters 29 *Chin*, 109 *Dan*, 110 *Dom*, 120 *Dut*, 240 *Ire*, 514 *Pol*, 615 *Rus*; *see also* Brothers and Sisters; Siblings
Slavery 1 *Afr*, 42 *Chin*, 57 *Chin*, 127 *Eng*, 128 *Eng*, 130 *Eng*, 131 *Eng*, 648 *Scot*, 656 *Sen*
Smuggling 213 *Gr*, 381 *Mex*, 458 *Mex*
Spanish 152 *Fr*
Sports/Baseball 3 *Arm*, 54 *Chin*, 61 *Chin*, 90 *Cub*, 201 *Ger*, 291 *Jap*, 293 *Jap*, 359 *Mex*, 376 *Mex*, 374 *Mex*, 384 *Mex*, 398 *Mex*, 461 *Mex*, 541 *P R*, 558 *P R*, 570 *P R*, 611 *Rus*, 627 *Rus*, 682 *Tai*
Sports/Basketball 358 *Mex*, 408 *Mex*, 463 *Mex*, 557 *P R*
Sports/Bull Fighting 72 *Chin*
Sports/Football 375 *Mex*, 551 *P R*
Sports/Soccer 426 *Mex*
Sports/Swimming 223 *Hung*
Sports/Tennis 91 *Cub*, 435 *Mex*
Storytelling 30 *Chin*
Superstitions 192 *Ger*, 695 *Viet*
Survival 6 *Arm*, 13 *Aus*, 34 *Chin*, 121 *Dut*

Toys 66 *Chin*

Urban Life 111 *Dut*, 218 *His*, 221 *His*, 257 *It*, 456 *Mex*, 529 *P R*, 531 *P R*, 537 *P R*, 540 *P R*, 542 *P R*, 552 *P R*, 561 *P R*, 571 *P R*, 593 *P R*, 597 *P R*, 617 *Rus*, 632 *Rus*, 716 *W I*

Values 81 *Chin*, 122 *Dut*, 164 *Fr*, 166 *Ger*, 178 *Ger*, 202 *Ger*, 207

Gr, 217 *His*, 266 *It*, 278 *It*, 357 *Mex*, 507 *Pol*, 521 *Pol*, 554 *P R*, 556 *P R*, 565 *P R*, 624 *Rus*, 642 *Rus*
Vietnamese War 693 *Viet*

War 167 *Ger*, 424 *Mex*
Weather 635 *Rus*
West, American 38 *Chin*, 43 *Chin*, 126 *Eng*, 258 *It*, 523 *Pol*, 530 *P R*, 644 *Rus*
Witchcraft 346 *Mex*
Women 74 *Chin*, 322 *Jap*, 370 *Mex*, 388 *Mex*, 621 *Rus*; *see also* Women's Rights
Women's Rights 4 *Arm*, 607 *Rus*
Working World 13 *Aus*, 53 *Chin*, 107 *Cze*, 155 *Fr*, 158 *Fr*, 159 *Fr*, 174 *Ger*, 233 *Ire*, 248 *Ire*, 261 *It*, 262 *It*, 270 *It*, 274 *It*, 277 *It*, 279 *It*, 343 *Lith*, 348 *Mex*, 388 *Mex*, 420 *Mex*, 441 *Mex*, 451 *Mex*, 524 *Port*, 546 *P R*, 547 *P R*, 592 *P R*, 606 *Rus*, 607 *Rus*, 608 *Rus*, 617 *Rus*, 626 *Rus*, 638 *Rus*, 664 *Sw*, 692 *Ukr*; *see also* Careers
World War II 180 *Ger*, 265 *It*, 285 *Jap*, 310 *Jap*
Writing 222 *Hung*, 661 *Sw*